MEMORY TECHNIQUES
for science students

(A must for XI, XII,IIT,CPMT,NET and other science students)

NEERJA ROY CHOWDHURY

FUSION BOOKS

Published by : **Fusion Books**
X-30, Okhla Industrial Area, Phase-II
New Delhi-110020
Phone : **011-40712200**
E-mail : sales@dpb.in
Website : www.dpb.in
Printed by :

MEMORY TECHNIQUES FOR SCIENCE STUDENTS
by : Neerja Roy Chowdhury

This Book Is Dedicated To My Family.

ACKNOWLEDGEMENTS

There are many people I would like to acknowledge for their support and help. I wish to thank Mr. Biswaroop Roy Chowdhury for his support and inspiration. I'm grateful to Yashika and Rupali Agarwal who helped me by giving their invaluable suggestions. I thanks to Madhvi for her unconditional emotional support and friendship.

I'm thankful to Ms. Saroj Arora for her empathetic listening and guidance. I must thank Devyani, Pawan Garg, Shankar Singh Koranga, Mr. Praveen Java and Malti for their generosity and readiness to support.

Thanks to my students for encouraging me to write a book on a subject that is regarded as the toughest of its kind. I thank Ms.Madhu for her instant guidance.

I have the good fortune of having a very understanding and loving family. This book is in nothing but the result of my parents', sisters' and brother's belief in my abilities. My special thanks to Poonam, Seema and Rinky. And finally a big thanks to Anjul for being the most wonderful brother in the whole world.

INDEX

QUICK RECALL TECHNIQUES FOR FORMULAE

MNEMONICS FOR MEMORISING BIOLOGY

GENERAL

INTRODUCTION

If you think poor, you will be poor,
If you think rich, you will be rich,
If you think success, you will be successful,
If you think goodwill, you will attract good will,
If you think friendship, you will attract friends,
If you think love, you will be loved,

It is so. It is in accordance with the law of consistency. It can not be otherwise.

The above lines show the power of thought. It is well said-thoughts rule the world. Our thoughts are mental pictures; these mental pictures guide us throughout our life.

In the context of studies, we can say our thoughts about the subject define the amount of learning. Of course, thoughts can make us efficient and effective to produce any result in our studies, but they must be very strong and organised. If it is not so; they will take us nowhere. Mostly students resort to 'Rote Memorisation'. In rote memorisation thoughts are most of the time unorganised and students blindly mug up the answers. They repeat the things until the material is registered in their subconscious mind. Whenever they are asked a question answer will flow out. This type of memory is known as 'Rote' or parrot like memory. Although, this is also a method to learn the things but it is boring. Remember, how many times we commit to ourselves that today we will memorise all the tables or biological diagrams or periodic table or equations or maps or long question answers, and then we mug them up blindly; hours later when we try to recollect we find ourselves confused and frustrated.

Let's now face the fact that rote memorisation is time

consuming, boring and inefficient. In rote memorisation you are required to take more and more revisions and still there is no guarantee of perfect and timely recall.

Though hard work is a must and there is no substitute for hard work, however in today's competitive era you can not win with hard work alone. The number of educated job seekers is increasing day-by-day but the proportions of jobs are not. So, apart from hard work, smart work is needed. Just think one person is spending days breaking a rock with hammer and another fixes a dynamite and removes it in few seconds. One is working hard and another smart. Who is showing better performance? Obviously the person who is taking advantage of scientific technology. Similarly, there are sciences that help us understand the functions and features of our brain. If you learn these sciences, you can be very successful in your studies and work. These techniques are based on visualisation and they can make learning easy. According to these techniques you can keep any information perfectly in your mind if you can convert it into mental pictures.

Remember, the subjects which you assume are easy to understand and remember are those which are easy to imagine. For example; stories in language books or some interesting historical event.Most of the students spend lesser time on these subjects since they are confident about these imaginable subjects. But what about the subjects like chemistry, biology, maths, physics etc.? Students spend more and more time on these subjects, they work hard on such subjects in school, tuition and at home and still they are not confident about the perfect recollection of what they study.

Reason is simple-retention of the material in these subjects is difficult because almost every information is in abstract form. Students feel helpless in retaining as they have never seen it in their practical life. And hence it is unimaginable for them.

Hence, we can say that the difference between easily understood and remembered subjects and so called gruesome subjects is of imagination.

If we are able to apply imagination and creatively on abstract subjects too, we can understand and remember them with great easiness and fun.

This book is an endeavour to lessen the trouble students' face in memorising chemistry, biology, math's and physics formulae. This book aims at showing how to apply creatively of thought and fun on these subjects.

This is my effort to show students a different and effective way of learning by converting the abstract data into visual pictures. Although my focus in this book is on chemistry, biology and mathematical and physics formulae but the same principles can be applied to memorise other subjects too.

I will be happy even if a single student is benefited by this book. I heartily welcome your precious suggestions to improve upon my work in future. I can be contacted at-

neerjatomar@yahoo.com

Neerja Roy Chowdhury

CHAPTER-1

KNOW THE MIND'S POTENTIAL AND POWER

According to researches human mind's potential is limit less. More specifically many scientists say that average human being uses only 10% of his mind. From these two statements emerges an exciting implication- the human potential awaits to be released.

If we are using only 10% of your mind power, then think what possibilities are in releasing just another 50% of our potential. If we're already successful and effective using only 10% of our mind power then what height we can raise to if we can release the total reserved power within us? Miracles lie ahead.

Mind consists of the conscious and subconscious, which together have an extraordinary power. It has been known that behind the conscious mind lies the subconscious. The subconscious consists of a vast bank of information and capacities. The subconscious acts as a huge sponge which absorbs information from most important to totally unimportant and nothing escapes.

A very simple example which all of us would have experienced shows the efficiency of our subconscious - many a times we try to remember a name and cannot. But when we engage in some other work that is totally different from remembering that name it springs to mind.

This example shows that our mind is capable of keeping anything we put in. Problem does not lie with the capability of our brain but with our inefficiency to tap the unlimited power of our mind.

How can we tap this potential and enable ourselves to learn better and remember more effectively? Is there anything that can develop accelerated learning that is- super memory? Is there any method that can be learnt so that we can release the stored super energy we have, which will enable us to achieve the seemingly impossible.

The answer is an unconditional YES.

LEARN MNEMONICS TO MEMORISE FAST

CHAPTER-2

MNEMONICS

A WAY TO SIMPLIFY MEMORISATION

'Mnemonics' is used to describe memory techniques which we are about to learn. If we look for dictionary meaning of mnemonics, it will be defined as 'an artificial aid to memory'.

How do mnemonics aid memory? We shall understand it later in the book. Before this we should concentrate on how we retain information.

There are two types of retention-

- **Short Term**
- **Long Term**

The **short term** retention is the one in which an idea is in the brain but has not been properly coded and due to this it is easily forgotten.

For example- vocabulary memorised by 'rote memory' is the example of 'short term memory'. We remember and forget since blind memorisation does not enable our brain to encode the vocabulary.

In **long term** retention, the idea is completely coded, filed and stored, and it will remain in the mind for years, if not for life.

Mnemonics is a way of storing the information in the mind by creating artificial interest in it. It makes deep impression of the information to be memorised in the mind. The basic principles of mnemonics are --Visualisation and Association.

CHAPTER- 3

VISUALISATION

THINKING IN SENSORY IMAGES

We talk in words to communicate most of the time but have we ever realised that our brain understands the language of pictures?

Thinking consists of manipulations and rearrangement of memory images. These memory images are gathered through our senses. Since in human beings vision is the most important information rich sense, it makes visual thinking extremely powerful and important. The other senses also produce memory images, which can similarly be the basis of thought. We can form the mental images of sound, feelings and taste in the same way as visual images.

According to the law of visualisation we can remember anything perfectly if we are able to see it in our brain. It is because the impact of pictures is found to be profound on our brain.

Visualisation is the technique of using imagination purposefully. In visualisation we use our imagination to focus on a particular topic in order to concentrate on that topic perfectly. Positive visualisation results in positive situations, circumstances, people etc. The more positive energy we put into our visualisation, the more positive results we get.

Whenever we visualise, we should take care of the following things-

Movement: Making the pictures moving and three dimensional in form.

Rhythm: Putting rhythm in the mental pictures to make them outstanding.

Humour: Having fun with memory by making the pictures funny, absurd and ridiculous.

Substitution: Increasing the probability of recollection by substituting a meaningful image for a boring or abstract material.

Colour: Making mental images as colourful as possible.

Exaggeration: Exaggerating the images, shapes and sizes to make them more memorable.

HOW DOES VISUALISATION HELP IN STUDIES?

- **It forces us to focus attention on what we are trying to learn.**
  Visualisation makes it impossible not to pay attention. We are forced to concentrate and hence we absorb information more effectively.
- **Visualisation gives meaning to what we try to learn.**
  Many a times we find a meaning inherent in the information we are trying to learn but this is not the case always. In case information is not meaningful to our brain we can impose meaning on the material through visualisation to make it more memorable since something that is meaningful is more memorable.
- **It makes us more organised.**
  Along with the technique of association or linking (in the next chapter) visualisation makes us more organised. W e k n o w that life is easier when we have a system for placing and finding things. For example if all the books are arranged alphabetically in a rack, it is easier to find any book of our choice. In the same manner if all the information is organised in our brain it is easier to find particular information instantly.
- **Visualisation enhances creativity and makes us feel confident.**
  We often think that we're not creative. No need to worry about that since we all are born creative and anyone can create such funny images.This way of learning our subjects not only improves our creativity but also makes us feel better since now we feel comfortable in recalling what we have memorised.

CHAPTER-4

LINKING SYSTEM

ASSOCIATION

Linking system is a very powerful way of remembering the information. In this system we hook together the information which we are trying to learn. This is also known as 'association method'.

We can memorise speeches, articles, points of our subject, shopping list etc. by linking system. This is also known as ' dominoes technique' because as in the domino effect one event causes a series of similar other events to happen one after the other in the similar way we link the words in such a manner that one word causes the next word to happen and so on . It also helps us remember the series of words easily and effectively.

Take an example of randomly selected words-

Table
Pen
Bomb
Library
Field
Tea
Building
Snakes
Petrol Pump
Vegetables
Flag
Leaders
Bridge
Curtains
Market
Cloth Mill
Badminton
River

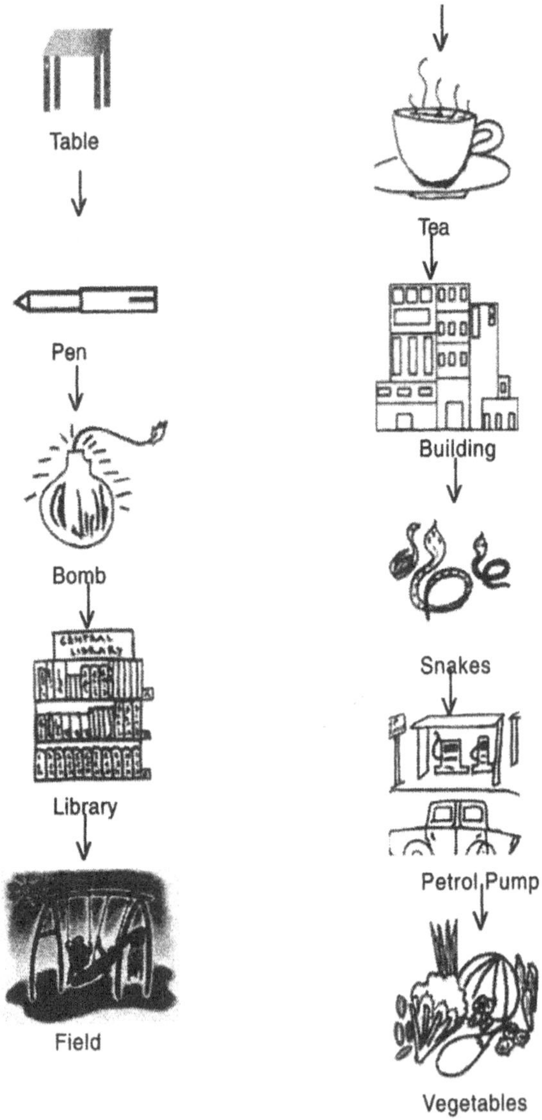
Table
Pen
Bomb
Library
Field
Tea
Building
Snakes
Petrol Pump
Vegetables

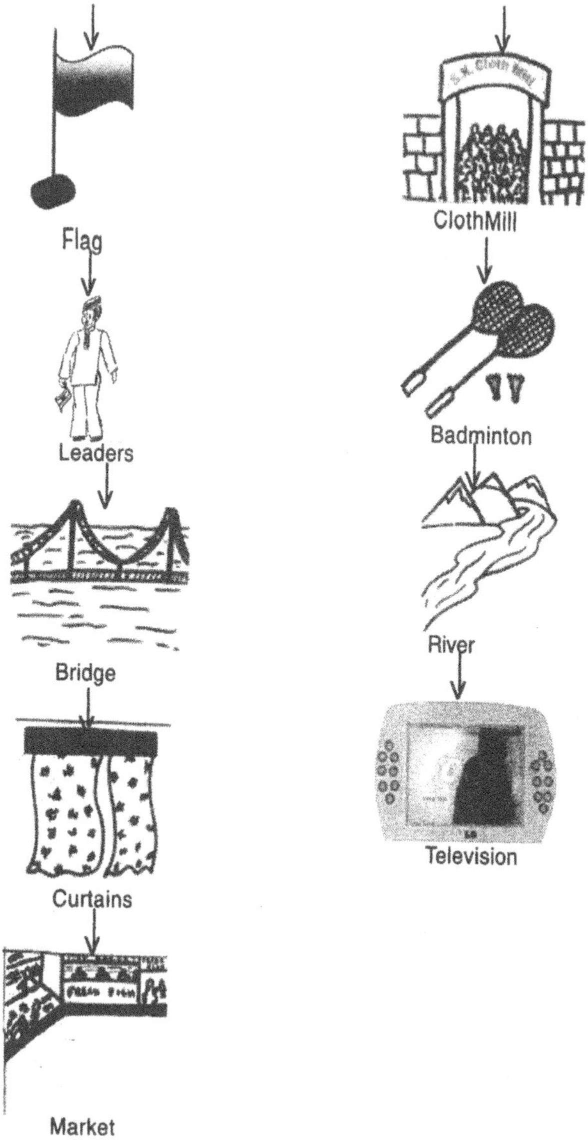
Flag
Leaders
Bridge
Curtains
Market
ClothMill
Badminton
River
Television

Have you seen all the objects? Yes. Now, you can visualise and link them like this-

You're sitting on a **table** with a **pen.** Now you pinch a **bomb** with the pen. As the bomb blasts, the room gets converted into a **library.** There is a **field** outside the library where **tea** is being distributed .After taking tea you come to a **building**. There are many **snakes** in the building. You're scared so you go to **petrol pump** to bring petrol to kill them. But there you find petrol man is selling **vegetables** instead of petrol. As you pick up a vegetable it suddenly gets converted into a **flag.** Seeing flag many **leaders** come there. You follow the leaders and reach a **bridge.** There is a big **curtain** on the bridge. As you shift the curtain you see a **market** behind it. There is a **cloth mill** in the market. As you enter the cloth mill you find there a lot of **badminton** instead of clothes. Taking a badminton you reach a **river** to play. But what do you see? **Televisions** are floating in the river.

Now see this story as colourful as you can in your mind and try the exercise on the next page.

TEST

Recall all the words in same order.	Take any lesson from any subject where you need to remember 10-20 points in the same order. List the points down and memorise them through link system.
1. 2. 3. 4. 5. 6. 7. 8. 9. 10. 11. 12. 13. 14. 15. 16. 17. 18. 19. 20. 21. 22.	1. 2. 3. 4. 5. 6. 7. 8. 9. 10. 11. 12. 13. 14. 15. 16. 17. 18. 19. 20. 21. 22.

CHAPTER- 5

SUBSTITUTION

PERSONALISED MEANING SYSTEM

Was it difficult to memorise the words given in the previous chapter? No, it was not difficult. Since the words were visual, we associated them and remembered. But every word or idea which we need to memorise is not visual. We can not imagine abstract ideas or words. To overcome this hurdle substitution- word concept emerges. Substitution -word concept can be applied to any seemingly abstract material.

This is also known as personalised meaning system. In personalised meaning system or substitution we give a picture to an abstract word by replacing it with a similar sounding 'visual' word. So whenever we need to visualise a particular abstract word we see its personalised meaning i.e. similar sounding word's picture in mind.

How to do

- Substitution can be used when we hear or see a word that seems abstract or intangible to us.
- Whenever we hear or see such intangible word, we should think of something that sounds like or reminds us of that abstract word.
- Then we should picture it in our mind.

For example

Generally the name of a person or place can not be pictured in our mind. So we can make their substitution as-

Ramanujan	-	Ram (new) jam
Italy	-	Idly*(a south Indian dish)

By using a bit of imagination, we can form conscious association between these words.

Some more examples of substitution are given below, as they are used in the book-

Lithium	-	Lichee
Hydrogen	-	Balloon of hydrogen
Rubidium	-	Ruby Bhatia* (actress)

Carbon Car

We are benefited by substitution concept in many ways-

- Pictures, Substitute words, thoughts or phrases that we use remind us of the intangible material.
- Process of finding a substitute word for something forces us to think about it.
- It improves our concentration and makes us remember what we normally would not do.

The perceptions brought in by the five senses are first treated or worked upon by the faculty of imagination, and it is the material of intellectual faculty. Imagination is the intermediary between perception and thought.

- Aristotle

CHAPTER- 6

ACRONYM METHOD

Acronym is a familiar method to learn something easily. In this method we take the first letter of each word in a list of words we want to remember and make a word or phrase by joining them.

For example:

If you want to remember the names of the five great lakes- Huron, Ontario, Michigan, Erie and Superior.

By acronym method we take H from Huron, O from Ontario M from Michigan, E from Erie and S from Superior. If we bring together all the first letters and arrange them we can make one meaningful word and it is HOMES.

This technique enhances creativity and makes us feel confident since we are now more comfortable in recalling the organised information.

In the coming chapters we shall discuss the other fast learning techniques.

CHAPTER- 7

MINOR PEG SYSTEM

A peg system can be compared to a wardrobe containing some hangers on which we hang our clothes. The hangers on which we hang our clothes never change but the clothes vary. In the similar way pegs or memory codes never change but the information we attach to each peg may vary. Peg systems are very useful in organising and remembering the information. These pegs are also used to assign pictures to the numbers, so that we may retain them better.

Minor peg system is covered by two subsystems-

- **The Number Rhyme System**
- **The Number Shape System**

Minor peg system covers only twenty pegs or memory codes and hence it is known as 'Minor' peg system'.

The Number Rhyme System

We will cover first ten pegs in Number Rhyme System. In this system we assign image of a word to a number that rhymes with the sound of the number.

For example peg for one could be bun, sun, run etc. Here we have to choose one visual word that seems appropriate to us. We can choose any image which we like. Here rhyming words for first ten numbers are given-

1 One - Sun
2 Two - Shoe
3 Three - Tree
4 Four - Door
5 Five - Knife
6 Six - Vicks
7 Seven - Heaven
8 Eight - Plate
9 Nine - Wine
10 Ten - Hen

Numbers and their rhyming word images

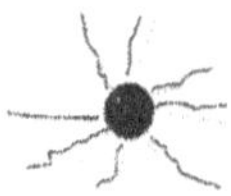
One

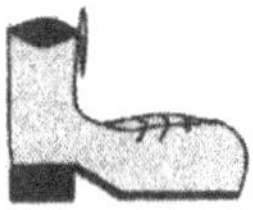
Two

Three

Four

Five

Six

Seven

Eight

Nine

Ten

The Number Shape System

We have formed pegs or codes up to 10 using rhyming method. Now we shall form pegs up to next 10 digits using number shape system. In this system we concentrate on the shape of a particular digit to form its corresponding memory code or peg.

Number	Concentrate on	Shape looks like
11	1	Stick
12	2	Duck
13	3	Heart
14	4	Chair
15	5	Hook
16	6	Hockey
17	7	Lamppost
18	8	Spectacles
19	9	Lollypop
20	10	Bat and Ball

Now, again concentrate on the shape of digits given to form the mental images of the numbers. These images are the pegs from 11 to 20.

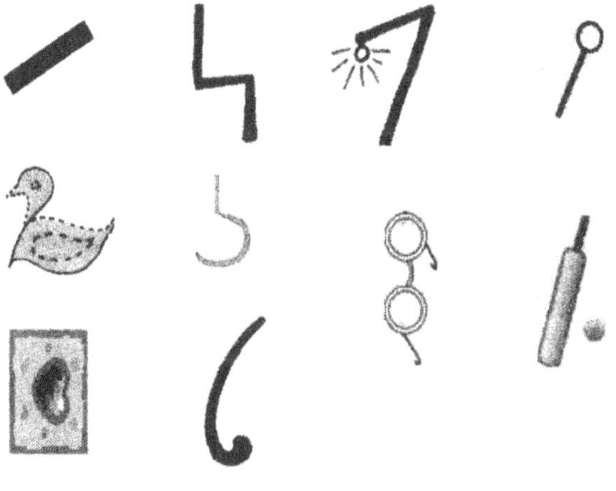

TEST

Recollect the images for the given numbers and draw them in the provided space.

11 --

12 --

13 --

14 --

15 --

16 --

17 --

18 --

19 --

20 --

Using rhyming system we can memorise any word list up to 10. In the same manner combining rhyming and shape system we can remember any list up twenty words.

Apart from memorising the list we can also use the minor system to convert any number from 1 to 20 into a mental image.

Memorising random word list

Now, you're ready to memorise this twenty word list using the first twenty pegs sequentially-

1. Chair	2. Pillow	3. Cup
4. Plate	5. Sheet	6. Mobile
7. Newspaper	8. Rubber	9. Aeroplane
10. Hospital	11. Radio	12. Garden
13. Hotel	14. Bus	15. Shop
16. Bread	17. Computer	18. Tiger
19. Light	20. Snake	

To remember this list you require to associate the word with the memory code (peg) of number as-

1. Sun - Chair

Imagine: You're putting **sun** on the **chair.**

2. Shoe - Pillow

Imagine: You're sleeping by putting **shoes** under your head instead of **pillow.**

3. Tree - Cup

Imagine: There is a **tree** in your compound on which **cups** are hanging.

4. Door- Plate

Imagine: Your **door** is like a big **plate**.

5. Knife - Sheet

Imagine: You're cutting a **sheet** with a big **knife**.

6. Vicks - Mobile

Imagine: You're rubbing **Vicks** on your **mobile** to make it shiny.

7. Heaven - Newspaper

Imagine: All gods and goddesses in the **heaven** are busy in reading **newspaper** to get the news of the world.

8. Plate - Rubber

Imagine: You are cleaning your **plates** with a **rubber**.

9. Wine - Aero plane

Imagine: **Aero plane** is getting jerks since pilot has drunken **wine**.

10. Hen -Hospital

Imagine: In **hospital** all doctors are **hens**.

11. Stick-Radio

Imagine: You are hanging your **radios** on a **stick**.

12. Duck -Garden

Imagine: You are in a beautiful **garden** which is full of **ducks**.

13. Heart - Hotel

Imagine: You are entering a **heart** shaped **hotel**.

14. Chair -Bus

Imagine: A **chair** is attached to a **bus**.

15. Hook -Shop

Imagine: A **shop** is hanging on a big **hook**.

16. Hockey -Bread

Imagine: You are mashing **breads** with a **hockey** stick.

17. Lamppost -Computer

Imagine: You are working on a **computer** under a **lamppost**.

18. Specs - Tiger

Imagine: A **tiger** is wearing **specs.**

19. Lollypop - Light

Imagine: **Light** is coming out of a **lollypop**.

20. Bat and ball- Snake

Imagine: You are playing cricket with a **snake** in hand instead of a **bat**.

Now you should close your eyes and visualise the items in the list from 1 to 20 with the help of the pegs once again. While visualising you should see the pictures vivid, moving and try to attach emotions in them.

TEST

Recall the twenty word list you have recently memorised.

1. ------------------	2. ------------------	3. ------------------
4. ------------------	5. ------------------	6. ------------------
7. ------------------	8. ------------------	9. ------------------
10. ------------------	11. ------------------	12. ------------------
13. ------------------	14. ------------------	15. ------------------
16. ------------------	17. ------------------	18 ------------------
19. ------------------	20. ------------------	

Time taken ....
Score.......

CHAPTER- 8

MAJOR PEG SYSTEM
Phonetic method

Minor System is quite interesting and successfully describes how to convert any number up to 20 into a mental image. But we are not confronted with numbers up to 20 only. We know we may require remembering a list beyond 20 or we may require converting a number beyond 20 into a picture. For example - there are 108 elements in the periodic table. And if we memorise their atomic numbers through visualisation, we will require the pictures for numbers beyond twenty. Minor system is not going to help us beyond the number twenty, so we need another system to maintain our efficiency.

Major System is the ultimate tool to help us maintain our efficiency and convert any number into a mental picture.

Let me describe the concept of major system. This is known as major system because it can convert any number into a picture. Its scope is wide .This is also known as phonetic system because codes or picture are based on phonetic sounds.

In the first step we will assign a consonant or consonant sound to each number from 0 to 9-

Number		Consonant
0	-	s,z
1	-	t,d
2	-	n
3	-	m
4	-	r
5	-	L
6	-	j,g,ch,sh
7	-	k
8	-	v, f
9	-	p, b

We need not remember them by rote; here some special associations are given which will help us to retain the consonants corresponding to the numbers-

0 - 0 is round and sun is also round so we represent '0' by the first letter of sun i.e. S. The first letter of the word 'Zero' is Z. So Z also represents '0'.

1- Letters t and d both have one down stroke.

2- If we invert 2, it will look like n

3- If we invert 3, it will look like m.

4- The letter r is the last letter of the word four.

Or

In Hindi we write 4 as ४ which resembles to 'r'.

5- Visualise a hand with five fingers spread out, the index finger and thumb forms L shape.

6- The letter j is the mirror image of 6. G looks like 6. In Hindi 6 is pronounced as 'chay' and its sound corresponds with the sounds of sh and ch.

7- Two 7 make one K.

8- Two V make one 8.The small letter f has two loops similar to the number 8.

9- The letters p and b are the mirror images of 9.

We can notice that we have used only 17 consonants to name the digits from 0 to 9. No vowel is included in the list.

Whenever we have to form a picture word or code of a number we can use the vowels and remaining consonants as **'fillers'**.

Take an example of 69. In 69 ,6 and 9 are represented by J and P respectively; **6 9 = J P**

To give it a meaning, mentally run through vowels a-e-i-o-u, start from the first vowel 'a'. If insertion of vowel 'a' gives it a meaning then ok otherwise go to next vowel and so on.

69= JeeP.

'Jeep' seems appropriate so we select jeep for 69, but we can choose our own word if we wish.

Example: 21 NeT

Here 2 means n and 1 means t, we have deliberately put a vowel 'e' between them to make it meaningful.

***Example: 74 CaR(kar)**

In this example, we have taken C for 7 instead of K since 'C' sounds like K here. In phonetic system sound is the main consideration.

***Example: 66** JudGe

In this example although we have put d between J and G;but it will not be considered because 'd' is silent here.

Example: 482 R -V -N

RaVaN

Example: 2161 N -T -CH -T

NaTCHaT

Key Images for first 100 numbers

Key images for first 100 numbers are given. We can also form our own key images-

1.	Tie	2.	Eno	3.	Ma
4.	Ray	5.	Hall*	6.	Jaw
7.	Key	8.	Fee	9.	Bee
10.	ToeS	11.	DaD	12.	DeN
13.	DaM	14.	DeeR	15.	TaiL
16.	TaJ	17.	DecK	18.	DeaF
19.	TaP	20.	NaSa	21.	NeT
22.	NaN/NuN	23.	NaMe	24.	NaRi
25.	NaiL	26.	NaaG	27.	NecK
28.	NaVy	29.	NiB	30.	MeSs
31	MaT	32.	MooN	33.	MaMa

34. MaRe	35. MaiL	36 MatCh
37. MiKe	38. MaFia	39. MaP
40. RoSe	41. RaT	42. RaiN
43. RaM	44. RoaR/ReaR	45. RaiL
46. RaJa	47. RacK	48. RooF
49. RoPe	50. LaSe/LaSsi	51. LoTa
52. LawN	53. LaMa/LiMe	54. LawyeR
55. LiLy	56. LodGe*	57. LaKe
58. LeaF	59. LaB/LaP	60. CheSs*
61. ChaT	62. ChaiN	63. JaM
64. JaR	65. JaiL	66. JudGe*
67. JacK	68. CheF	69 ChiP
70. CaSe	71. CaT	72. CaN
73. ComB*	74. CaR	75. CoaL
76. CaGe/CaSh	77. CaKe	78. CaFe
79. CuP/CaP	80. FuSe	81. FaT/FooT
82. FaN	83. FoaM	84. FiRe
85. FiLe	86. FiSh	87 ForK
88. FiFe/FuFa	89. V.I.P.	90. BuS
91. BaT	92. BuN/BeaN	93. BeaM
94. BaR	95. BeLL*	96. BaG
97. BiKe	98. BeaF/PuFF*	99. BaBy
100. TheSiS		

Note: In **Hall** only one 'L' will be considered since as we hear sound of only one L . The same rule is applicable to **Chess, Bell**

and **Puff**

In **Comb** 'b' will not be considered since it is silent. Same rule is applied for **Judge**.

How to recall the codes

Suppose we need to recall the image for 92. We have to think aloud in our mind B--------N and that is Bun. Initially we have to practice these codes for few days but with time proficiency will come in immediate recollection of the image for any given code.

The major system is very useful in remembering atomic numbers, melting points, boiling points, historical dates, telephone numbers etc.

Exercise

Practice the major system and fill up the following blanks.

1	----------------	2	----------------	3	----------------
4	----------------	5	----------------	6	----------------
7	----------------	8	----------------	9	----------------
10	----------------	11	----------------	12	----------------
13	----------------	14	----------------	15	----------------
16	----------------	17	----------------	18	----------------
19	----------------	20	----------------	21	----------------
22	----------------	23	----------------	24	----------------
25	----------------	26	----------------	27	----------------
28	----------------	29	----------------	30	----------------
31	----------------	32	----------------	33	----------------
34	----------------	35	----------------	36	----------------
37	----------------	38	----------------	39	----------------
40	----------------	41	----------------	42	----------------
43	----------------	44	----------------	45	----------------

46 ----------------	47 ----------------	48 ----------------
49 ----------------	50 ----------------	51 ----------------
52 ----------------	53 ----------------	54 ----------------
55 ----------------	56 ----------------	57 ----------------
58 ----------------	59 ----------------	60 ----------------
61 ----------------	62 ----------------	63 ----------------
64 ----------------	65 ----------------	66 ----------------
67 ----------------	68 ----------------	69 ----------------
70 ----------------	71 ----------------	72 ----------------
73 ----------------	74 ----------------	75 ----------------
76 ----------------	77 ----------------	78 ----------------
79 ----------------	80 ----------------	81 ----------------
82 ----------------	83 ----------------	84 ----------------
85 ----------------	86 ----------------	87 ----------------
88 ----------------	89 ----------------	90 ----------------
91 ----------------	92 ----------------	93 ----------------
94 ----------------	95 ----------------	96 ----------------
97 ----------------	98 ----------------	99 ----------------
100 ----------------		

CHAPTER -9

VALUE SYSTEM

In value system we imagine the value of a number to give it a picture

Example:

1. One

One means a single entity. So we can compare 'one' with 'Prime minister' or 'Raja of a country.

So in value system we can imagine one as Raja.

In the like manner, we can convert other numbers into images Some images are given below-

Number	Mental Image
1	Raja
2	Couple
3	Three monkeys of Gandhiji
4	Four wheeler
5	Pandavas*(Mahabharat)
6	Sixer of Sachin
7	Seven colours of Rainbow
8	Octopus
9	Nine Planets
10	Ten heads of Ravana* (Ramayan)
11	Football team
12	One dozen Banana
13	A Horrible Event
14	14 Year Ram's exile to Jungle
15	15thAugust, Independence Day
16	A sweet sixteen girl
17	7' Up (cold drink) tin
18	Voter's age
19	1900 Century, Your birthday
20	Rs 20 lakh lottery ticket

Go through all the mental images two-three times and try the exercise.

TEST

Mention the images of the following numbers by the value system.

1	------------------	2	------------------
3	------------------	4	------------------
5	------------------	6	------------------
7	------------------	8	------------------
9	------------------	10	------------------
11	------------------	12	------------------
13	------------------	14	------------------
15	------------------	16	------------------
17	------------------	18	------------------
19	------------------	20	------------------

Time taken.........

score................

MEMORISE CHEMISTRY WITH MNEMONICS

CHAPTER - 10

SOME BASICS OF PERIODIC TABLE

There are more than 100 elements in the modern periodic table. An English physicist Mosley showed that the atomic number is a more fundamental property of an element than its atomic mass. The position of an element in the periodic table depends on its atomic number. The horizontal rows are known as 'periods'. Elements having similar outer electronic configurations of their atoms are grouped in vertical columns. These are referred as 'groups' or families. There are altogether seven periods, and eighteen groups numbered from 1 to 18.

TYPES OF ELEMENTS (S-d-p-f)

Elements are grouped into four blocks viz. s-block, p-block, d-block and f-block depends upon the type of atomic orbital that is being filled with electrons. The salient features of the four types of elements are marked in the periodic table.

S-block elements

The elements of group 1 and group 2 belong to s-block elements.

Group 1 elements are known as **'Alkali metals'** and group 2 elements are known as **'Alkaline metals'**.

By value system we know that 1 means Raja for us and 2 means couple. Now, we can remember the above mentioned names by linking 1 i.e. Raja to Alkali and 2 i.e. couple to Alkaline. But before doing that we need to personalise the words Alkali and Alkaline. We can do that by thinking **Alkali as 'Akali Political party leaders'** and **Alkaline as 'Kaline'**. Here kaline is a Hindi word means carpet .Now, we can think that Akali party leader is trying to be Raja i.e. Prime Minister of our country in order to link Group 1 with the word Alkali.

In the process to memorise that Group 2 which is known as Alkaline Metals we can think that a couple is sitting on a Kaline.

The D-Block elements

These are the elements of group 3 to 12 in the centre of the periodic table.

The familiar name for d-block elements is **transition elements**.

To remember the group number covered by d-block elements, we can think that next 10 groups after s-block are covered by d-block elements. These 10 groups are making a long road on which **transport** i.e. **transition** of metals are going on.

The P-block element

Remaining groups belong to p-block. Now we know that group 1 and group 2 belong to s-block, next 10 groups i.e. from 3 to 12 belong to d-block. We can mentally calculate that the remaining i.e. (18-(2+10) =6) 6 groups from 13 to18 belong to p-block.

In p-block group 17 is halogen group. Now in order to personalise 17, we can think of it as **'7' Up tin'** by using value system and we can substitute **halogens** as **'hello saying gentlemen'**. Now we can link them together by visualising that the hello saying gentlemen are drinking 7' Up cold drink.

The F-block element

The two rows of elements at the bottom in the periodic table come under the f-block elements.

It is easily remembered so we need not put extra effort to memorise it.

Remember the sequence (s-d-p-f) by SanDwich effect

In the periodic table we notice that sequence of blocks is not s-p-d but it is **s-d-p**. To remember this think of a big Sandwich which you are eating in the period of chemistry.**S**an**d**wich will make you sure that first s-block and than d-block elements occur in the periodic table. P-block elements come after that. F-block elements are lying on the bottom of periodic table is easily memorable.

S -block D- block P- block

Group Period	1	2		3	4	5	6	7	8	9	10	11	12	13	14	15	16	17	18
1	1 H																		2 He
2	3 Li	4 Be												5 B	6 C	7 N	8 O	9 F	10 Ne
3	11 Na	12 Mg												13 Al	14 Si	15 P	16 S	17 Cl	18 Ar
4	19 K	20 Ca		21 Sc	22 Ti	23 V	24 Cr	25 Mn	26 Fe	27 Co	28 Ni	29 Cu	30 Zn	31 Ga	32 Ge	33 As	34 Se	35 Br	36 Kr
5	37 Rb	38 Sr		39 Y	40 Zr	41 Nb	42 Mo	43 Tc	44 Ru	45 Rh	46 Pd	47 Ag	48 Cd	49 In	50 Sn	51 Sb	52 Te	53 I	54 Xe
6	55 Cs	56 Ba	*	71 Lu	72 Hf	73 Ta	74 W	75 Re	76 Os	77 Ir	78 Pt	79 Au	80 Hg	81 Tl	82 Pb	83 Bi	84 Po	85 At	86 Rn
7	87 Fr	88 Ra	**	103 Lr	104 Rf	105 Db	106 Sg	107 Bh	108 Hs	109 Mt	110 Ds	111 Rg	112 Uub	113 Uut	114 Uuq	115 Uup	116 Uuh	117 Uus	118 Uuo
*Lanthanoids			*	57 La	58 Ce	59 Pr	60 Nd	61 Pm	62 Sm	63 Eu	64 Gd	65 Tb	66 Dy	67 Ho	68 Er	69 Tm	70 Yb		
**Actinoids			**	89 Ac	90 Th	91 Pa	92 U	93 Np	94 Pu	95 Am	96 Cm	97 Bk	98 Cf	99 Es	100 Fm	101 Md	102 No		

F- block

CHAPTER - 11

ELEMENTS IN EACH GROUP

There are in all 18 groups in the periodic table each containing some elements. A chemistry student is required to memorise strongly which group a particular element belongs to; what is its atomic number and what its valency is in order to answer the questions related to that element. But it is a tedious job to remember the atomic number and valency or group number for an element .Especially if we try to remember them through blind repetition or rote memory because even after repeating them many times, we cannot guarantee a perfect long time memory. If we don't repeat them for some time (say for one week) we start confusing.

We shall learn in this chapter how to apply creativity and imagination to memorise the elements within a group. After memorising the elements in a group we do not require to memorise their valencies, since we can easily tell the valency for an element if we know the group which it belongs to.

To remember atomic numbers of elements, we shall refer to the next chapter.

Here group numbers are converted by value system into visual pictures. Personalised words or substitutes for elements are shown against them in the next column. Now we shall start with group 1.

Symbol	Group1	Raja
Li	Lithium	Lichee
Na	Sodium	Soda-bottle
K	Potassium	Pot
Rb	Rubidium	Rubi Bhatia* (actress)
Cs	Cesium	Scissors
Fr	Francium	Frock

To remember group 1 elements we shall link all the elements with Raja i.e.group number1.

Imagine: Visaualise that a **Raja** is eating **lichee (Li)** and drinking **soda (Na)** by pouring it into a beautiful **pot (K)**. He is also enjoying dance of **Rubi Bhatia*(Rb)** who is holding **scissors (Cs)** and wearing a **Frock (Fr)**.

Symbol	Group 2	Couple
Be	Beryllium	Borolene*(cream)
Mg	Magnesium	Maggie
Ca	Calcium	Calcium Sandoz tablets
Sr	Strontium	Strong
Ba	Barium	Bar
Ra	Radium	Radio

Imagine: A **couple (group2)** is holding **borolene* (Be)**. As they squeeze it **Maggie (Mg)** comes out instead of cream. Now they are eating Maggie mixed with small white **calcium sandoz tablets (Ca)**.They are getting **strong (Sr,**see the muscles growing) as they eat it. Then they go to a **bar (Ba)** where they begin to dance to the music of a **radio (Ra)**.

Symbol	Group 3	Three Monkeys
Sc	Scandium	Scan
Y	Yttrium	Stone-bow
La	Lanthanum	Lan+ Ac=Lanka*
Ac	Actinium (Ac)	

For the second element Yttrium we will visualise the symbol **Y** as **stone-bow**. Next two elements have been personalised by giving them a new word Lanka *(Shri Lanka,a country) which has been produced by joining the first letters of the two elements Lanthanum and Actinium.

Imagine: Imagine that **three monkeys (group3)** are **scanning (Sc)** Shri **Lanka* (La** and **Ac)** with a **stone bow (Y)**.

Symbol	Group 4	Four Wheeler
Ti	Titanium	Titanic
Zr	Zirconium	Jerk
Hf	Hafnium	Half
Rf	Rutherfordium	Rutherford Scientist

Imagine: Four wheels (group4) are being fixed to the **titanic ship (Ti)** by the scientist **Rutherford (Rf)**. Now ship is propelling but it is getting **jerks (Zr)** and thus is broken into two **half (Hf)** pieces.

Symbol	Group 5	Pandavas
V	Vanadium	Van
Nb	Niobium	New Bomb
Ta	Tantalum	Tent
Db	Dabnium	Dabur Co.Products

Imagine: See in your mind that **five pandavas (group5)** are going in a **van (V)**.Somebody throws a **new bomb (Nb)** on them. They enter a big **tent (Ta)** to protect themselves where they find a lot of **dabur products (Db).** See dabur hajmola, dabur honey etc. in your imagination.

Symbol	Group 6	Sixer of Sachin
Cr	Chromium	Crow
Mo	Molybdenum	Mobile
W	Tungsten	Tongue

Imagine: Sachin Tendulkar is playing cricket.He hits a **sixer(group6)**.See the ball is going up in the sky. Oh! The ball hits a **crow (Cr)** who is talking on a **mobile (Mo)**. As the ball hits the head of the crow its **tongue (W)** comes out.

Symbol	Group 7	Rainbow
Mn	Manganese	Mango
Tc	Technetium	Technician

Imagine: On a **rainbow (group7), mangoes (Mn)** are being fitted to make it more beautiful by a **technician (Tc).**See technician is hanging in the sky.

Symbol	Group 8	Octopus
Fe	Iron	Iron
Ru	Ruthenium	Rath* (Chariot)
Os	Osmium	Osho*(Indian Philosopher)

Imagine: Visualise an **octopus (group 8)** is driving a **rath* (Ru)** made up of **iron(Fe)** in which **Osho* (Os)** is sitting.

Symbol	Group 9	Nine Planets
Co	Cobalt	Bolt
Rh	Rhodium	Road
Ir	Iridium	I ride

Imagine: You are **riding (I ride, Ir)** on a **planet (group9)** and making a **road (Rh)** of big **bolts (Co)** in the space.

Symbol	Group 10	Ravan with ten heads
Ni	Nickel	Knickers
Pd	Palladium	Paddle
Pt	Platinum	Plate

Imagine: Ravan* (group10) is wearing **knickers (Ni)** and trying to move **paddle (Pd)** with his feet which are **plate (Pt)** shaped.

Note: Hindi words are shown by a star* and their English meanings are written against them.

Symbol	Group 11	Football team
Cu	Copper	Cup
Ag	Silver	Silver
Au	Gold	Gold

Imagine: For **football team (group 11)** prize **cups (cu)** are made up of **silver (Ag)** and **gold (Au).**

Symbol	Group 12	Banana one dozen
Zn	Zinc	Zin*(ghost)
Cd	Cadmium	Candle
Hg	Mercury	Mercury

Imagine: You are eating **one dozen bananas (group12)**. As you peel a banana a **zin***(**zn)** comes out with a **mercury thermometer (Hg)** which is lightening like a **candle(Cd).**

Symbol	Group 13	Horrible Event
B	Boron	Bora*(Sack)
Al	Aluminum	Alloo*(Potato)
Ga	Gallium	Gali*(Street)
In	Indium	Indian
Tl	Thallium	Thal*(Big plate)

Imagine: You are very much **horrified (group13)** by seeing some **Indians (In)** standing in a scary **gali (Ga)** beating **big thals *(Tl)** vigorously. To protect yourself you hide yourself in a **bora*(B)** which contains rotten **alloos* (Al).** Feel the stinking smell of potatoes.

Symbol	Group 14	Ram's exile for 14 year
C	Carbon	Car
Si	Silica	Sita*(Ramayan)
Ge	Germanium	Jam
Sn	Tin	Tin
Pb	Lead	Lead pencil

Imagine: Visualise Lord Ram is going for **14 years exile (group14)** in a **car (C)** along with **Sita*(Si).** People are offering them big **tins (Sn)** of **jam (Ge)** to eat on the way to jungle. They are eating it with **lead pencils (Pb).**

Symbol	Group 15	15th, August
N	Nitrogen	Night
P	Phosphorus	Fox with pores
As	Arsenic	Sainik*(Soldier)
Sb	Antimony	Aunty
Bi	Bismuth	Biscuit

Imagine: On **15th, August (group15)**, at **night (N)**, **fox with pores (P)** is doing Independence Day parade wearing **sainik* (As)** uniform and an **aunty (Sb)** is giving **biscuits (Bi)** to her for this nice job.

Symbol	Group 16	Sweet sixteen girl
O	Oxygen	Ox

S	Sulphur	Sulpha*(Cigar Pipe)
Se.	Selenium	Saloon
Te	Tellurium	Talcum powder
Po	Polonium	Pole

Imagine: A **sweet sixteen girl (group16)** sitting on an **Ox (O)**. Ox is smoking **sulpha* (S)** made up of a **pole (Po)** and is sitting in a **saloon(Se)**.The saloon man is trying to put out the fire in the sulfa by pouring **talcum powder (Te)** on it.

Symbol	Group 17	7' Up tin (Cold drink)
F	Fluorine	Floor
Cl	Chlorine	Clown
Br	Bromine	Broom
I	Iodine	Iodex

Imagine: A **Clown (Cl)** emerges as you throw your **7' Up tin (group17)** on the **floor (F)**. You beat him with a **broom (Br)** for his arrival. When he gets injured you apply **Iodex (I)** on his wounds.

Symbol	Group 18	Voters age
He	Helium	Helen* (Actress)
Ne	Neon	Knees
Ar	Argon	Gun
Kr	Krypton	Cry
Xe	Xenon	Zenut Aman*(Actress)

Imagine: In an election during the **voting (group18)** actress **Helen* (He)** is dancing on her **knees (Ne)** and **crying (Kr)** badly as **Zenut* Aman (Xe)** is coming towards her to kill her with a **gun (Ar)**.

A lot of information about periodic table has been provided in this chapter in a very organised and imaginable form. Now, this is the time to revisualise them in order to strengthen their impressions on your brains. Visualise them two three times and be ready to answer the questions in the following exercise.

TEST

Answer the following questions

Q1 Write down the elements of group 15.

Q2. Which element belongs to which group?

Element	**Group No.**
Y	---------------
Pt	---------------
W	---------------
Ag	---------------
Cd	---------------
Hg	---------------
Sb	---------------
Bi	---------------
Ga	---------------
Mg	---------------
Ca	---------------

Q3. Answer the following questions in **Yes/No.**

a) Pd and Hg belong to same group	Yes/No
b) La and Ac belong to Group 4	Yes/No
c) Nb and Ta are from same group	Yes/No
d) Sn and Sb lie in group 16	Yes/No
e) Mg, Sr and Ba belong to Group 2	Yes/No
f) He, Ne, Argon, Kr are proceeded by Rf	Yes/No

CHAPTER -12

ELEMENTS AND THEIR ATOMIC NUMBERS

In the previous chapter we learned how to remember the elements in a group. In this chapter we'll deal with the elements and their corresponding atomic numbers. Now we shall learn how to recall atomic number of an element in a moment.

Below a list of elements along with their corresponding atomic numbers has been provided. Against it another column, containing the personalised words for atomic numbers and elements is given. All you need to do here is to link the personalised words of atomic number to that of element. You will find it very funny and this fun in turn will give you an efficient recalling. That recalling system will be perfect----so perfect that you will recall in a moment the atomic number of any element or vice versa.

Element	Atomic No.	Element	At.No.
H	1	Hydrogen balloon	Sun
He	2	Helen*(actress)	Shoe
Li	3	Lichee	Tree
Be	4	Borolene*(cream)	Door
B	5	Bora*(sack)	Knife
C	6	Car	Vicks
N	7	Night	Heaven
O	8	Ox	Plate
F	9	Floor	Wine
Ne	10	Knees	Hen
Na	11	Soda Bottle	Stick
Mg	12	Maggie	Duck
Al	13	Alloo*(potato)	Heart
Si	14	Sita*(Ramayan)	Chair
P	15	Fox	Hook
S	16	Sulfa* (cigar pipe)	HockeyStick
Cl	17	Clown	Lamppost
Ar	18	Gun	Specs
K	19	Pot	Lollypop

Ca	20	Calcium tablets	Bat and Ball
Sc	21	Scan	Net
Ti	22	Titanic Ship	Nun
V	23	Van	Name
Cr	24	Crow	Nari
Mn	25	Mango	Nail
Fe	26	Iron	Naag
Co	27	Bolt	Neck
Ni	28	Knickers	Navy
Cu	29	Cup	Nib
Zn	30	Zin*(ghost)	Mess
Ga	31	Gali*	Mat
Ge	32	Jam	Moon
As	33	Sainik* (soldier)	Mama
Se	34	Saloon	Mare
Br	35	Broom	Mail
Kr	36	Cry	Match
Rb	37	Rubi Bhatia * (actress)	Mike
Sr	38	Strong	Mafia
Y	39	Stone Bow	Map
Zr	40	Jerk	Rose
Nb	41	New Bomb	Rat
Mo	42	Mobile	Rain
Tc	43	Technician	Ram
Ru	44	Rath* (chariot)	Roar/Rear
Rh	45	Road	Rail
Pd	46	Paddle	Raja
Ag	47	Silver	Rack
Cd	48	Candle	Roof
In	49	Indian	Rope
Sn	50	Tin	Lassi/Lase
Sb	51.	Aunty	Lota
Te	52	Talcum powder	Lawn
I	53	Iodex	Lane/lime
Xe	54	Xenut Aman* (actress)	Lawyer
Cs	55	Scissors	Laloo/Lily
Ba	56	Bar	Lodge
La	57	Lantern	Lake

Ce	58	--------	--------
Pr	59	--------	--------
Nd	60	--------	--------
Pm	61	--------	--------
Sm	62	--------	--------
Eu	63	--------	--------
Gd	64	--------	--------
Tb	65	--------	--------
Dy	66	--------	--------
Ho	67	--------	--------
Er	68	--------	--------
Tm	69	--------	--------
Yb	70	--------	--------
Lu	71	--------	--------
Hf	72	--------	--------
Ta	73	--------	--------
W	74	--------	--------
Re	75	--------	--------
Os	76	--------	--------
Ir	77	--------	--------
Pt	78	--------	--------
Au	79	--------	--------
Hg	80	--------	--------
Ti	81	--------	--------
Pb	82	--------	--------
Bi	83	--------	--------
Po	84	--------	--------
At	85	--------	--------
Rn	86	--------	--------
Fr	87	--------	--------
Ra	88	--------	--------
Ac	89	--------	--------
Th	90	--------	--------
Pa	91	--------	--------
U	92	--------	--------
Np	93	--------	--------
Pu	94	--------	--------
Am	95	--------	--------
Cm	96	--------	--------
Bk	97	--------	--------
Cf	98	--------	--------

Es	99	---------	--------
Fm	100	---------	--------
Md	101	---------	--------
No	102	---------	--------
Lr	103	---------	--------
Rf	104	---------	--------
Db	105	---------	--------
Sg	106	---------	--------
Bh	107	---------	--------
Hs	108	---------	--------
Mt	109	---------	--------

Here it can be noticed that we have personalised the atomic no. up to 20 using rhyming and shape method and after that we have resorted to phonetic method. Although we have the option to use only phonetic system throughout the list of atomic number but here we have also used rhyming and shape method codes since they are easier to remember.

Now this is the time to link the information. Elements can be linked with their atomic numbers in any way; we do not need to be logical. The more abnormal and funny the association is, the more memorable it will be.

1. Hydrogen (H)

Sun-Hydrogen balloon

Imagination: A big and beautiful **hydrogen balloon** is going up in the sky towards the **sun**.

2. Helium (He)

Shoe- Helen

Imagination: Helen* is dancing wearing **shoes** around her neck.

3. Lithium (Li)

Tree-Lichee

Imagination: You are plucking red tasty **lichees** from a **tree**.

4. Beryllium (Be)

Door-Borolene

Imaginagion: You are applying **borolene** on the **door** of your room.

5. Boron (B)

Knife- Bora*(sack)

Imagination: You are cutting a **bora*** with a **knife**.

6. Carbon (C)

Vicks- Car

Imagination: You are rubbing **Vicks** on your brand new **car** to make it shiny.

7. Nitrogen (N)

Heaven-Night

Imagination: At **night** you are seeing dreams of **heaven**.

8. Oxygen (O)

Plate-Ox

Imagination: You are feeding an **ox** from a big **plate**.

9. Fluorine (F)

Wine- Floor

Imagination: Today you're washing your **floor** with **wine**.

10. Neon (Ne)

Hen-Knees

Imagination: A **hen** is sitting on your **knees**.

11. Sodium (Na)

Stick- Soda

Imagination: You are drinking **soda** with **stick**.

12. Magnesium (Mg)

Duck-Maggie

Imagination: You are feeding your **duck** with **maggie**.

13. Aluminum (Al)

Heart-Alloo*

Imagination: **Alloo*** is **heart** shaped.

14. Silica (Si)

Chair-Sita

Imagination: **Sita** ma is sitting on a **chair**.

15. Phosphorus (P)

Hook-Fox with pores

Imagination: You are hanging a **fox with pores** on a big **hook**.

16. Sulphur (S)

Hokey-Stick-Sulpha*(Cigar pipe)

Imagination: You are smoking **hockey stick** as a **sulpha***.

17. Chlorine (Cl)

Lamppost-Clown

Imagination: A **clown** is entertaining you under a beautiful **lamppost**.

18. Argon (Ar)

Specs-Gun

Imagination: Some people are attacking you wearing **specs** with **guns**.

19. Potassium (K)

Lollypop-Pot

Imagination: You are putting **lollypop** in a **beautiful pot** before guests.

20. Calcium (Ca)

Bat&Ball-Calcium sandoz tablets

Imagination: All **cricket players (bat-ball)** are taking **calcium sandoz tablets.**

21. Scandium (Sc)

Net-Scan

Imagination: You are **scanning** a big **net** before playing.

22. Titanium (Ti)

Nun-Titanic ship

Imagination: Nuns are dancing on the **titanic ship**.

23. Vanadium (V)

Name-Van

Imagination: On a **van** you are writing your **name**.

24. Chromium (Cr)

Nari-Crow

Imagination: A **crow** is teasing a **nari**

25. Mangenese (Mn)

Nail-Mango

Imagination: You are eating a **mango** by peeling it with your big

nails.

26.Iron(Fe)

Naag -Iron

Imagination: You are playing with a **naag** made up of **iron.**

27. Cobalt (Co)

Neck-Bolt

Imagination: You are fixing a big **bolt** around your **neck**.

28. Nickel (Ni)

Navy-Knickers

Imagination: All **navy soldiers** are parading wearing **knickers**.

29. Copper (Cu)

Nib-Cup

Imagination: You're scratching a **cup** with a sharp **nib**.

30. Zinc (Zn)

Mess-Zin*(ghost)

Imagination: A **Zin*** is serving you food in a **mess**.

31. Gallium (Ga)

Mat-Gali

Imagination: You are spreading **mats** in a **gali**.

32. Germanium (Ge)

Moon-Germs

Imagination: Moon is **swallowing** the **germs** from the earth.

33. Arsenic (As)

Mama-sainik

Imagination: Mamaji* is fighting wearing a **sainik** dress.

34. Selenium (Se)

Mare-Saloon

Imagination: A hair dresser in a **saloon** is trimming the tail of a **mare**.

35. Bromine (Br)

Mail-Broom

Imagination: You're sweeping **mails** with a **broom**.

36. Krypton (Kr)

Match -Cry

Imagination: People are **crying** while watching a **match**.

37. Rubidium (Rb)

Mike-Ruby Bhatia* (actress)

Imagination: Ruby Bhatia* is speaking on a **mike**.

38. Strontium (Sr)

Mafia-strong

Imagination: A group of **strong mafias** is coming.

39. Yttrium (Y)

Map-Stone Bow

Imagination: You are practicing shots by hitting stones on a **map** with a **stone bow**.

40. Zirconium (Zr)

Rose-Jerk

Imagination: You are getting **jerks** when you're touching a **rose**.

41. Niobium (Nb)

Rat -New bomb

Imagination: A **rat** is making a cat frightened with a **new bomb**.

42. Molybdenum (Mo)

Rain-Mooly*(Radish)-denim

Imagination: It's **raining** so **mooly*** is wearing **denim** clothes.

43. Technetium (Tc)

Rama-Technician

Imagination: Lord **Rama** has come as a **technician** in your home.

44. Ruthenium (Ru)

Roar-Rath*

Imagination: You are going on **rath*** and the horses are **roaring** like a lion.

45. Rhodium (Rh)

Rail-Road

Imagination: A **rail** is running on the **road**.

46. Palladium (Pd).

Raja* -Paddle

Imagination: A **raja*** is very fat so he is **paddling** in order to get in shape.

47. Silver (Ag)

Rack -Silver

Imagination: You're putting your books in a **rack** made up of **silver**.

48. Cadmium (Cd)

Roof-Candles

Imagination: On your **roof** you are fixing **candles**.

49. Indium (In)

Rope -Indian

Imagination: **Indians** are tying **ropes** on the boundary of the country so that no enemy can enter it.

50. Tin (Sn)

Lassi-Tin

Imagination: You're drinking **lassi** in a **tin**.

Here there are fifty examples on how to link atomic number to its corresponding element name. Rest of the atomic numbers can also be easily memorised by linking them with their respective elements.

Please do link them here-

51. Antimony (Sb)

Lota-Aunty

Imagination:- --

----

52. Tellurium

Imagination:- --

----

53. Iodine

Imagination:- --

----

54. Xenon

Imagination:- --

----

55. Cesium

Imagination:- --

----

56. Barium

Imagination:- --

----

57. Lanthanum

Imagination:- --

58.Cerium

Imagination:- --

59.Praseodymium

Imagination:- --

60.Neodymium

Imagination:- --

61.Promethium

Imagination:- --

62.Samarium

Imagination:- --

63.Europium

Imagination:- --

----

64. Gadolinium

Imagination:- --

----

65. Terbium

Imagination:- --

----

66. Dysprosium

Imagination:- --

----

67. Holmium

Imagination:- --

----

68. Erbium

Imagination:- --

----

69. Thulium

Imagination:- --

----

70. Ytterbium

Imagination:- --

----

71. Lutetium

Imagination:- --

----

72. Hafnium

Imagination:- --

----

73. Tantalum

Imagination:- --

----

74. Tungsten

Imagination:- --

----

75. Rhenium

Imagination:--

----

76. Osmium

Imagination:- --

----

77. Iridium

Imagination:- --

----

78. Platinum

Imagination:--

----

79. Gold

Imagination:--

----

80. Mercury

Imagination:- --

----

81. Thallium

Imagination:- --

----

82. Lead

Imagination:- --

----

83. Bismuth

Imagination:- --

84.Polonium

Imagination:- ---

85.Astatine

Imagination:- ---

86.Radon

Imagination:- ---

87.Francium

Imagination:- ---

88.Radium

Imagination:- ---

89.Actinium

Imagination:- ---

90.Thorium

Imagination:- ---

91.Protactinium

Imagination:- ---

92.Uranium

Imagination:- ---

93.Neptunium

Imagination:- --

94.Plutonium

Imagination:- --

95.Americium

Imagination:- --

96.Curium

Imagination:- --

97.Berkelium

Imagination:- --

98.Californium

Imagination:---

99.Einsteinium

Imagination:- --

100.Fermium

Imagination:- --

101.Mendelevium

Imagination:- --

102.Nobelium

Imagination:- --

103.Lawrencium

Imagination:- --

104.Rutherfordium

Imagination:- --

105.Dubnium

Imagination:- --

106.Seaborgium

Imagination:- --

107.Bohrium

Imagination:- --

108.Hassium

Imagination:- --

109.Meitnerium

Imagination:- --

Revision Time: Do revise the atomic numbers of elements through visualisation two three times, then appear for the exercise and check out your score.

Note: * shows the word is taken from Hindi language.

TEST

1. What is the atomic number of the following elements.

Elements Name	Atomic No.
Fr	....
Y	....
Ac	....
Nb	....
Ni	....
Hg	....
Ti	....
N	....
Se	....
Kr	....
Mn	....
Ru	....
Sr	....
K	....
Sb	....
Sn	....
Ri	....
O	....
Mo	....

Score: Assign1 mark for each correct answer

2. Here some atomic numbers have been given.Can you tell which elements belong to them-

Atomic No.	Element. No.
49	....
30	....
29	....
21	....
11	....

Time taken..........

Score........

CHAPTER -13

VARIATION IN PROPERTIES ACROSS PERIODS

In this chapter we will memorise the variation in the properties of elements left to right across period. A list of properties in a period along with their variation is provided below-

1. **Atomic Number** - Increases

2. **Atomic Weight** - Generally increases

3. **Nuclear Charge** - Increases

4. **Effective Nuclear Charge** - Generally Increases

5. **Valency** - From left to right across a period valency with respect to oxygen increases from 1 to 7, while that with respect to hydrogen rises from 1 to 4 and then falls to 1.

6. **Atomic Radii** - Generally Decreases

7 **Ionic Radii**- Generally Decreases

8. **First Ionisation Energy**- Generally Increases

9. **Electron Affinity** - Generally Increases

10.**Electro Negativity**- Generally Increases

11. **Atomic Volume**- Generally Decreases

12. **Metallic Character**- Decreases

13. **Reactivity of Metals** - Generally Decreases

14. **Reducing power of Metals**- Generally Decreases

15. **Volatility of Metals**- Generally Increases

16. **Lattice energy of Metals**- Generally Increases

17. **M.P and B.P of Metals** - Generally Increases

18. **Density of Metals**- Generally Increases

19. Basic Nature of Oxides - Decreases

20. Basic of Nature of Hydrides - Generally Decreases

21. Basic Nature of Hydroxides - Generally Decreases

22. Acidic Nature of Oxides - Increases

23. Acidic Nature of Hydrides - Generally Increases

24. Acidic Nature of Hydroxides - Generally Increases

25. Hydration Energy of Elements- Generally Increases

26. Oxidising power of Non-Metals- Generally Increases

Now we shall convert all the abstract properties given here into visual pictures by substitution method.To do this first we shall observe the original name then we shall compare it with something imaginable.All the substitutes which we are going to use to memorise the variation in properties are given below along with their actual meaning or originals.Sometimes the reason why a particular substitute has been taken is mentioned in the bracket although there is no hard and fast rule to stick to these substitutes and story only.We are free to form our own story with our own substitutes. We can take the substitutes and story given in this chapter as an example.

	Original	**Compared with(substitute)**
1	At.No.	Number of Students in a class
2	At. Weight	Weight of the class
3	Nuclear Charge	Fee students are paying
4	Effective Nuclear Charge	Effect of the fee on the teacher
5.	Valency	Bells(as val is similar in sound with bell)
	oxygen valency 1-7	Deck (D=1, K=7, by phonetic method and oxygen is substituted by an Ox.
	Hydrogen valency 1-4-1	Tarat (T=1, R=4, T=1 by phonetic and hydrogen is substituted by hydrogen balloon.
6.	Atomic Radii	A circle(as radii is the

	characteristic of a circle)
7. Ionic Radii	Onions(ionic is compared with onion)
8 Ist Ionisation Energy	Energy required to peel the Ist layer of an onion
9. E -Affinity	Attraction for electrons
10. E-Negativity	Bitterness due to electrons
11. Atomic Volume	Volume of the voice
12. Metallic Character	Students made up of metal
13 Reactivity of Metal	Activeness of metal students
14. Reducing power of metal	Redness on the face of metal students
15. Volatility of Metals	Voltmeter made up of metal
16. Lattice energy of Metals	Net made up of metal(as lattice is net -like)
17. M.P. and B.P of Metals	Melting of Metal Students(B.P.will be automatically recalled with melting)
18. Density of Metal	Metal students in Den
19. Basic Nature of Oxides	Bossy nature of ox
20. Basic Nature of Hydrides	Bossy nature of the hydras
21. Basic Nature of Hydroxides	Bossy nature of the hydra sitting on Ox
22.Acidic nature of oxides	Acid drinking Ox
23. Acidic nature of Hydrides	Acid drinking Hydra
24. Acidic Nature of Hydroxides	Acid drinking Hydra sitting on an Ox
25.Hydration Energy of elements	Hydras getting energy from ration
26. Oxidising Power of non-metals	Non-Metal students getting ox as power

Mental Movie

Now we shall imagine a class environment and associate these substitutes to form a meaningful story.The central words or substitutes in the story are actually the representatives of the original concepts.This story will help you to recall the required original facts instantly and correctly .Here in this story whether the particular property is increasing or decreasing is mentioned in the bracket.

Visualise that a chemistry period is going to be start in a class.

Number of students (**At.No.**) are increasing in the class as more and more students are coming .

(At.no.Increases)

Class is being pressurised and unbalanced since weight of the class (**At. weight**) is increasing due to continuous arrival of students .

(At.weight Increases)

Every student who enters the class is paying a fee or charge to the teacher (**nuclear charge**). As the students are increasing collection of charge of the teacher is also increasing.

(Nuclear charge Increases)

Teacher starts laughing ha..ha...ha..seeing such great amount of money as the effectiveness of fee (**Effective nuclear charge**) is increasing.

(Effective nuclear charge Increases)

Teacher is very happy and he gives **bells (valency)** to the students. Students ring the bells.But what happened!. Ox and hydrogen balloons come out as music tones from the bells.As the ox comes out it starts dancing on the music of the **deck (1-7 valency of oxygen varies from 1 to 7)** and as the hydrogen balloons come out, they get burst and tarat (1-4-1) cards come out. It indicates that (**Valency of hydrogen increases from 1 to 4 then falls to 1).**

(Valency of O_2 varies from 1-7,valency of H_2 varies from 1-4-1)

A dancing environment is being created and every student in the class starts dancing in circles (**Atomic Radii**) . As the time precedes students get exhausted and dancing circles get smaller and smaller as students begin leaving the circle.

(At. radii Decreases)

Oh! What is this onions (**Ionic Radii**) automatically start growing in the circles. Bigger the circle, bigger the onion is . Since size of circles is reducing, so are the onions.

(Ionic radii Decreases)

Now see, that students start uprooting the onions. They want to eat onions so they peel them, Bigger the onion, easier it is to peel off the layer .Since size of onions is reducing with the reducing size of circles so more and more energy **(First Ionisation Energy)** is required to peel off the first layer of onions.

(First ionisation energy Increases)

·After eating the onions students start attracting the electrons **(E-affinity)**. See the electrons moving around their heads.

(E-affinity Increases)

Due to the electrons moving around their head, students start suffering from headache. They start shouting and get more and more bitter and negative **(E-negativity)** .

(E-negativity Increases)

Students are shouting and the volume of their voice**(Atomic Volume)** is getting down and down due to constant shouting.

(At. volume Decreases)

Teacher is annoyed with the students due to the noise in the class so he decides to punish the guilty students. He is says, "I will punish the metal students and other bossy students for the noise in the class."

Firstly he moves towards metal students and throws the rays on them to punish them . Due to the heat of rays metal students **(Metallic character)** start getting hurt.

(Metallic character Decreases)

Their reactivity starts decreasing **(Reactivity of metals)**constantly.

(Reactivity of metal Decreases)

Metals students get weaker and due to that the redness on their faces reduces. **(Reducing power)**

(Reducing power of metal Decreases)

Now teacher fixes a voltameter **(Volatility)** to measure the energy of the metal students and reading is going lower and lower as their power is decreasing .

(Volatility Decreases)

Teacher throw a net **(Lattice energy of metal)** to catch these weak metal students. He is tightens the net to get the students into a bundle. As the students try to get rid of the net they trap more into that.

(Lattice energy of metal Increases)

Students try their best to get rid of the net. They start melting their bodies rapidly to come out the net (**Melting Point, Boiling Point**).

(M.P.,B.P.of metal increase)

After coming out of the net they run to a den **(density of metal).** Number of metal students who are hiding themselves in the den is increasing .

(Density of metal Increases)

When all the metal students are gone teacher turns to the Ox(**Oxide**), the hydra(**Hydrides**), and the hydra sitting on the Ox(**Hydroxides**), to punish them since he feels that they are also guilty as these three students claim to be 'boss' of the class.

As the teacher throws rays on these three students to punish, they start crying and they sit on their knees on the floor , saying, " we are no more bossy **(Basic nature**) now .Please leave us".

(Basic Nature of Oxides,Hydrides, hydroxides - Decreases)

Teacher says," OK,I will not punish you by throwing rays but you have to sit on the floor and drink the acid **(Acidic nature)**. Ox, hydra and 'hydra sitting on ox' rapidly(**Acidic nature of oxides, hydrides and hydroxides**)drink the acid.

(Acidic nature of oxides,hydrides and hydroxides Increases)

Suddenly, hydra starts fainting due to the acid, as he is the weakest among the three. Teacher takes pity on hydra and gives him ration **(Hydration energy)** to eat. As the hydra eats ration he gets very much energetic.

(Hydration energy Increases)

Hydra gets so much energetic and enthusiastic that he starts throwing oxes towards the non- metal students.And non- metal students start catching them to enhance their ox power **(Oxidising power of non-metals**). After getting ox power they are very excited and clamouring with joy.

(Oxidising power of non-metals- Increases)

Now revisualise the whole story and try the exercise given on the next page.See if you can recall all the properties alongwith their variations.

TEST

Recall the properties along a period and also mention whether they are increasing or decreasing.

Property	**Increase/Decrease**
....	....
....	....
....	....
....	....
....	....
....	....
....	....
....	....
....	....
....	....
....	....
....	....
....	....
....	....
....	....
....	....
....	....
....	....
....	....
....	....
....	....
....	....
....	....
....	....
....	....
....	....
....	....
....	....
....	....
....	....
....	....
....	....
....	....
....	....
....	....

Time taken........

Score..........

Periodic properties in a group from top to bottom

On the basis of the properties along a period, variation in properties in a group from top to bottom can be known. Leaving the first two properties i.e. atomic number and atomic weight other properties follow the reverse trend for groups.

CHAPTER-14

MELTING POINT, BOILING POINT OF ELEMENTS

We have already learned how to memorise atomic number of various elements in a periodic table using number rhyme, shape and phonetic method. We shall apply the same principles to memorise the melting and boiling points of the elements. In our imagination we shall make special associations between elements and their melting and boiling points.

Element	Melting point (K)
Li	454
Na	371
K	336
Rb	312

Here we find that melting points are three digit numbers. By phonetic method we shall assign a particular alphabet to each digit. We shall convert the three digit numbers into as vivid and interesting images as possible. For example take 454

Replace the digits with alphabets – R-L-R

By inserting vowels between the alphabets we find that one of the imaginable possible words is- ROLLER. Here we shall not mind the extra L as it remains silent in the pronunciation.

Element	Melting point (K)	Image of number
Li	454	Roller
Na	371	Mukut
K	336	Mamaji
Rb	312	Matinee (Show)

Element	M.P
Li	454

Imagine: Lichees (Li) have started melting as you are trying to roll them into a **roller (454).**

Element	M.P
Na	371

Imagine: A **mukut (371)** is melting down as you're pouring **soda (Na)** on it.

Element	**M.P**
K	336

Imagine: Mamaji* (336) is trying melt down a **pot (K)** so that he can create another stylish pot out of it.

Element	**M.P**
Rb	312

Imagine: Ruby Bhatia* (Rb) has started melting with embarrassment when she saw herself in a **matinee (312)** show.

BOILING POINTS

Element	B.P (K)	**Image of number**
O	90.2	Besan* (gram floor)
N	77	Cake

Element	**B.P**
O	90.2

Imagine: An **ox (O)** is boiling **basen (90.2)** to prepare its food.

Element	**B.P**
N	77

Imagine: A **gentleman** in **night (N)** is boiling **cake (77)** to eat it.

CHAPTER- 15

QUANTITATIVE ANALYSIS

Physical Examination of the Mixture

The Physical examination of the unknown mixture involves the study of colour, smell and density. The test is not very reliable, but is certainly helpful to identify some coloured cations.

Experiment	Observation	Inference
a) Colour	Blue	Cu^{++}
	Greenish	Ni^{++}
	Light Green	Fe^{++}
	Dark Green	Cr^{++}
	Dark Brown	Fe^{+++}
	Pink Violet	Co^{++}
	Light Pink, Flesh Colour or dull earthy colour	Mn^{++}
	White shows absence of	Cu, Ni, Fe, Cr, Mn, Co,
b) Smell	Take a pinch of the mixture between your fingers and rub with a drop of water	
	Ammonical smell	NH_4^+
	Vinegar	CH_3COO^-
	Smell of rotten eggs	S^{2-}
c) Density	(i) Heavy	Salt of Hg^{++} Pb^{++} Ba^{++}
	(ii) Light fluffy powder	Carbonate
d) Delique-scence	Mixture absorbs moisture and becomes paste like	(i) If coloured may be $Cu(No_3)_2$ $FeCl_3$ (ii) If colourless may be $Zn(No_3)_2$ Chloride of Zn^{++}, Mg^{++} etc.

By Visualisation and link method we can retain this information simply as-

Colour: See yourself in your chemistry laboratory. Practical is going on and you are holding a **Cup (Cu^{++})** of **blue colour** which is containing the mixture to be tested. You are wearing **grass (green colour)** as **knickers (Ni^{++})** Now you pull out of your knickers a light green **iron (Fe^{++})** rod because a **crow (Cr)** has entered the laboratory. As you hit the crow with your green iron rod the crow becomes **dark green** in **colour** and your **iron rod** changes its colour to **dark brown**. Your face becomes **pink** at this and you get **voilent (voilet)** so you start emitting the **bolts (Co^{++})**. Bolts strike with a mango tree and **mangoes (Mn^{++})** of **light pink** colour start falling.Their **flesh (flesh colour)** i.e. pulp comes out and becomes of **earthy colour.**

Now, revisualise this funny incidence which happened to you while you were testing the mixture. Give special attention to the colours attached to captions.Now, focus on your imagination and try to recollect the colours of the following objects-

Object	**Colour**
Colour of Cup (Cu^{++})	Blue
Colour of grass knickers (Ni^{++})	Greenish
Colour of iron (Fe^{++}) rod	Light green
Colour of crow (Cr++)	Dark green
New colour of iron (Fe^{+++}) rod	Dark brown
Colour of bolts (Co^{++})	Pink violet
Colour of Mangoes (Mn^{++})	Light pink, Flesh colour, earthy colour.

Note: Here you can associate **ferrous (Fe^{++})** with light green colour and **ferric (Fe^{+++})** with dark brown colour.

Smell: You can easily and logically associate the smell observation with inferences. So no need to form any visualisation for this.

Density: You feel your mixture in the cup is very heavy. As you see the mixture you find some **mercury thermometer (Hg^{++})** and **lead pencils (Pb^{++})** and **ber*(jujube,Ba^{++})** in the mixture.

As you separate them from the mixture, your mixture gets light like powder. And you spread it on your **car bonnet(Carbonate).**

Deliquescence:

Visualisé that the mixture you are holding is absorbing moisture and has become paste like. Sometimes the paste is coloured and sometimes it is white. You give the paste to a Ni*(hair dresser) and-

(i) When paste is coloured the **Ni *(Hair dresser)** holding **Cup** (**$CuNo_3$**) starts colouring a **clown** sitting on a **Iron rod ($FeCl_3$)**.

(ii) When paste is white the **Ni*** paints a white **Zin*(ghost)** with it **($Zn(No_3)_2$)**

Visualise the entire sequence again and answer the questions in the exercise on the next page.

Note: *shows that the word is taken from Hindi language.

TEST

1. The colour of mixture to be tested is given, can you name the radicals which may be present in it.

Colour	Inference
Pink Violet	________
Greenish	________
Light green	________
Dark green	________
Blue	________
Bluish green	________
Dark brown	________
Earthy colour	________

2. Name the radicals which may be present if mixture is-

Heavy--------------------------------

Light fluffy powder----------------

3. The mixture absorbs moisture. It indicates the presence of -

If it is coloured ___________

If it is colourless___________

CHAPTER-16

SOME IMPORTANT PROCESSES

Bosch Process	Hydrogen
Caster Process	Manufacture of Na
Down Process	Manufacture of Na
Nelson Cell	Manufacture of NaOH
Parke's Process	Manufacture of Ag
Cupellation Process	Manufacture of Ag
Baeyer's Process	Manufacture of Al.
Carter Process	Manufacture of basic lead carbonate (White Lead)
Ostwald Process	Synthesis of HNO_3
Lead Chamber Process	Manufacture of H_2SO_4

In order to memorise what is being manufactured by a particular process we need to make a connection between the two.

1. Bosch Process	**Hydrogen**
Word	**Substitute**
Bosch	Boss
Hydrogen	Hydrogen balloon

Imagine : Now-a-days, your **boss** comes to the office in a big **hydrogen balloon**.

2. Caster Process	**Manufacture Na**
Word	**Substitute**
Caster	Cost
Na (sodium)	Soda bottle

Imagine: You are asking **cost** of a **soda bottle**.

3. Nelson cell	**Manufacture Na**
Word	**Substitute**
Nelson	Nelson Mandela

NaOH (Sodium Hydroxide)	Soap (As NaOH is known as caustic soda present in every soap)

Imagine: Mr. **Nelson Mandela** is manufacturing **soap** to wash slum area.

4. Down Process	**Manufacture Na**
Word	**Substitute**
Down	Underworld don
Na (sodium)	Soda bottle

Imagine: An **underworld don** is drinking **soda**.

5. Parke's Process	**Manufacture Ag**
Word	**Substitute**
Parke	Park
Ag (Silver)	Silver

Imagine: There is a **park** made up of **silver** in front of your home.

6 Cupellation Process	**Manufacture Ag**
Word	**Substitute**
Cupellation	Cup and lotion i.e. lotion in a cup
Ag (silver)	Silver

Imagine: You are cleaning your **silver** ornaments using **lotion in a cup**.

7. Baeyer's Process	**Manufacture Al**
Word	**Substitute**
Baeyer	Buying
Al (Aluminum)	Alloo* (potato)

Imagine: You are **buying alloo***.

8. Carter Process	**Manufacture white lead**
Word	**Substitute**
Carter	Carton
White lead	White colour lead pencils

Imagine: As you opened a **carton** you got a lot of **white** colour **lead pencils**.

9. Ostwald Process	**Synthesis of HNO_3**
Word	**Substitute**
Ostwald	Ostrich- world

HNO_3 (Nitric acid)	Ni *.(Hair dresser) and trick

Imagine: In the **world** of **Ostriches** a **ni*(hair dresser**) is playing **tricks** to cut their wings.

10. Lead Chamber Process	**Manufacture H_2SO_4**
Word	**Substitute**
Lead chamber	A chamber made up of lead pencils
H_2SO_4 (Sulphuric acid)	Sulpha* (cigar pipe) and fumes

Imagine: A **chamber** made up **lead pencils** is filled with **fumes** of a **sulfa*(cigar pipe).**

CHAPTER-17

SOME IMPORTANT ALLOYS

Bass	Cu +Zn
German silver	Zn +Ni+Cu
Bell metal	Cu + Sn
Gun metal	Cu +Sn+ Zn
Electron	Mg (95%) + Zn (5%)
Magnalium	Al + Mg
Solder	Pb + Sn

In order to memorise the metals and their alloys we need to relate what we want to remember to what we already know. To remember complicated instructions we need to visualise them rather then try to remember them in words. Proper visualisation enables us to hold more information in our working memory.

If, you think up a story that has personal meaning, you are much more likely to remember it. Here are the ways to visualise and elaborate the metals and their alloys.

1. Brass	**Cu +Zn**
Word	**Substitute**
Brass	Brass utensils
Cu (copper)	Cup
Zn (Zinc)	Zin* (ghost)

Imagine: A **Zin*(ghost)** is living in the **cup** made up of **brass**.

2. German silver	**Zn +Ni + Cu**
Word	**Substitute**
German	Germs
Silver	Silver
Zn + Ni (Zinc + Nickel)	Zini* (female zin)
Cu (copper)	Cup

Imagine: A **Zini* (Zn +Ni)** is coming out of a **cup** made up **silver** as it contains so many **germs(German)**.

3. Bell Metal	**Cu +Sn**
Word	**Substitute**
Bell metal	Bells
Cu + Sn (copper + tin)	Cushion

Imagine: A **cushion (Cu +Sn)** is being decorated with beautiful small **metal bells**.

4. Gun metal	**Cu + Sn + Zn**
Word	**Substitute**
Gun metal	A gun emitting metal
Cu + Sn	Cushion
Zn	Zin* (ghost)

Imagine: A **Zin*(Zn)** is protecting himself from the **metal** coming out of a **gun** by hiding himself behind a **Cushion (Cu +Sn).**

5. Electron	**Mg (95%) + Zn (5%)**
Word	**Substitute**
Mg (Magnesium)	Maggie
95	Ball (by phonetic)
5	Knife (by rhyme method)

Imagine: Electrons are revolving in **Maggie (Mg)** like **ball (95)** and a **Zin* (Zn)** is eating it with **Knife(5).**

6, Magnalium	**Al + Mg**
Word	**Substitute**
Magnalium	Maghna * (a girl)
Al + Mg	All Maggie

Imagine: Meghna (Magnalium) has eaten **all Maggie (Al+Mg)**.

7. Solder	**Pb + Sn**
Word	**Substitute**
Solder	Soldier
Pb + Sn	Pub and son i.e. son in a pub

Imagine: Your **son (Sn)** in a **pub (Pb)** is behaving like a brave **soldier (solder)** after drinking wine.

CHAPTER-18

PHYSICAL PROPERTIES OF GASES

The technique of visualising things in a dramatic way can be applied to remembering even the most mundane data such as physical properties of gases. Practice stretching you imagination by giving the physical properties of an element a more theatrical context. You can always find a connection if you look hard enough.

Chlorine

Greenish, yellow, suffocating smell, heavier than air, poisonous, fairly soluble in water, can be liquefied.

Imagine: Our picture word for chlorine is clown. Now we shall associate the properties of chlorine with clown like this-

You are confronted with a clown with a greenish yellow body and face. As you smell him you realise he is having a suffocating smell. You try to lift him but feel he is very heavy and very poisonous too as your hands start getting blue because of his poison. Somehow you manage to throw him in the water where he dissolves and get liquefied.

Whatever the plausibility of the story, any property of an element is easier to remember if it is stored in the brain as a part of a chain of cause and effect, actions and consequences.

CHAPTER -19

IMPORTANT ORES, REAGENTS AND CHEMICALS

Here some important ores, reagents and chemical names along with their common names are given. We shall link these common names with their chemical formulae.

1. Carnalite-KCl $MgCl_2$ $6H_2O$

If we try to memorise the formula of carnalite blindly , we may easily get confused in the formula after some time or even may forget it. In order to give it a space in the permanent memory we'll make a conscious association between the name and the formula like this-

Original	Substitution
Carnalite	Car
KCl	Pot-clown i.e.Clown with a pot
$MgCl_2$	Maggie-clown i.e. Clown with maggie
6	Jaw (By phonetic)
H_2o	Water

The **substituted form** of the formula will be-

Car = Pot-Clown.Maggie-Clown. Jaw .water

Now, we'll associate all the substitutes in such a way that will remind us of the actual formula.

Mental Picture: Visualise that in a **car a clown** is sitting holding **pot** containing **maggie** and throwing **water** out of his **jaw.**

2. Anti Knock Reagent-$(C_2H_5)_4$Pb

This is tetra ethyl lead

Original	Substitution
Anti knock reagent	To stop knocking
Tetra ethyl $(C_2H_5)_4$	Four thal*(Four big plates)
Lead	Lead pencil

The substituted form

To stop knocking=Four thal* .Lead pencil

Mental Picture: The engine of your vehicle is **knocking**, to stop it you are putting **four big thals** on it and pressing them with a big **lead pencil.**

3. Washing Soda- $Na_2Co_3.10H_2O$

This is sodium carbonate deca hydrate

Original	Substitution
Sodium-Carbonate	Soda-Carbonate i.e. some activity with soda on car bonnet
10	Hen (by minor system)
H_2O	Water

The substitution form

Washing = Soda and Car-bonnet.Hen.Water

Mental Picture: See that you are **washing** the **bonnet** of your **car** with **soda** and a **hen** is helping you by pouring **water** on it.

4. Dolomite- $CaCo_3.MgCo_3$

This is double salt of calcium carbonate and magnesium carbonate.

Original	Substitution
Dolomite	Doll (see Barbie doll)
$CaCO_3$	Calcium tablets and Car bonnet
$MgCO_3$	Maggie and Car bonnet

Substituted form

Doll=Calcium tablet and car-bonnet.Maggie and Car-bonnet

Mental Picture: A beautiful **Barbie doll** is sitting on a **car bonnet** and eating **calcium sandoz tablets** with **maggie** to enhance her beauty.

5. Kieserite- $MgSO_4.2H_2O$

This is magnesium sulphate and two water molecules.

Original	Substitution

Kieserite	Kesar* (Saffron)
Magnesium sulphate	Maggie in a sulpha*(cigar pipe)
,2	Eno (by phonetic method)
H_2O	Water

Substituted form

Kesar = Maggie in a sulpha* Eno. water

Mental Picture: You are decorating the **maggie** with **kesar** which is lying in **sulpha***. Now, you are eating it with **eno-water.**

6. Epsom Salt-$MgSO_4.7H_2O$

This is magnesium sulphate and seven water molecules.

Original	Substitution
Epsom	Ape
Magnesium sulphate	Maggie in a sulpha*(cigar pipe)
7	Key
H_2o	Water

Substituted form

Apes = Maggie in a sulpha .key .water

Mental Picture: An **ape** is mixing **water** with a **key** in **maggie** lying in a **sulpha*.**

7. Malachite-Cu_2O

This is copper oxide.

Original	Substitution
Mala chite	Mala* (Garland)chaat
Copper Oxide	Cup and Ox

Substituted form

Mala chaat = Cup and Ox

Mental Picture: An **ox** is eating **chaat** of **mala*** in a **big cup.**

8. Bauxite-$Al_2O_2.2H_2O$

This is Aluminum oxide and two molecules of water.

Substitute	
Bauxite	Boxer
Aluminum Oxide	Alloo* (potato) and Ox

2	Shoe (by minor system)
H_2o	Water

Substituted form

Boxer =Alloo* and ox .shoe.water

Mental Picture: A **boxer** is hitting an ox since it is eating his **alloo*** and drinking **water** in his **shoes.**

In the same way we can prepare our own list of reagent and chemicals which we need to memorise.We can make substitutes and funny associations and enjoy remembering. We can even do it mentally, to save the time.

Note: Our pictures for numbers up to twenty can either be from minor or major system. We can choose the picture according to our convenience in making associations.

For example-Picture for 10 can be both hen (by minor system) and dosa (by major system). We are free to choose any picture according to our convenience.

CHAPTER-20

STRUCTURAL FORMULAE

In this chapter, we shall understand how to apply creativity along with minor and major system on structural formulae to learn them. Here as example I have taken some formulae which students find difficult to remember. To facilitate the memorisation of structural formula we shall assume the numbering of benzene ring, as

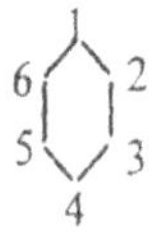

1. Aniline

Substitutes

Aniline	Anil Kapoor*(actor)
Amine (NH_2)	A mine

Students are very much clear about the benzene ring in the structure formula. So we need not memorise the benzene ring but we need to remember what is attached to benzene ring. For example here amine group (NH_2) is associated with benzene ring. So we shall associate the name of the formula i.e. aniline with the functional group attached with the ring.

Imagine: **Anil Kapoor** is dancing in a **mine** (NH_2).

2. Anthranilic Acid

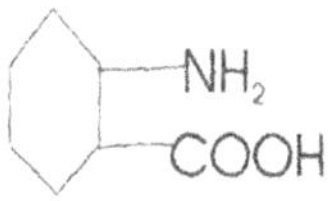

Substitutes

Ant-thr-anilic	Ant throws Anil Kapoor

NH_2(Amine)	Mine
COOH	HOOC= Hook
2-3	Name (by phonetic system)

Imagine: An **ant** is throwing **Anil Kapoor** into a **mine(NH_2)** and writing his **name (23)** with a big **hook (COOH)** outside the mine .Here name (2-3) will remind you that 2nd and 3rd positions of ring (counting from clockwise direction) have been occupied by NH_2 and COOH.

3. Phthalic Acid

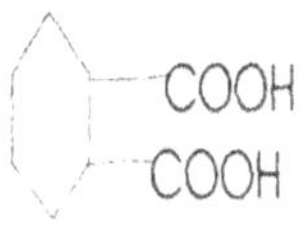

Substitutes

Phthalic	Pathology lab
COOH	HooK
23	Name (by phonetic)

Imagine : You are sitting in a **pathology lab** holding a big **hook** with which you're entering the **name (23)** of your clients.

Note: Here we are having only one attached group (Hook)and two positions (2 and 3) so both the positions will be occupied by the same group.

4. Sulphanilic Acid

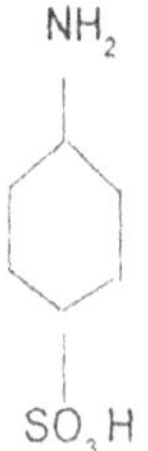

Substitutions

Sulph -anil-ic	Sulfa* smoking Anil Kapoor
Amine (NH_2)	Mine
Sul -phon-ic Acid	Cell Phone

1-4	Tear

Imagination: Anil Kapoor is smoking sulpha* in a **mine**, talking on his **cell phone** and shedding **tears (14).**

Note: Amine (NH_2) will occupy the first and sulphonic acid (SO_2H) will occupy the forth position from the anticlockwise direction.

5. Picric Acid

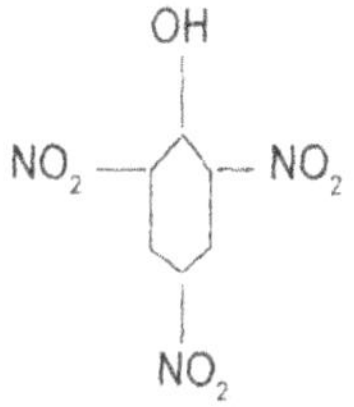

Substitution

Picric Acid	Picnic
OH (OL group)	Hole
No_2 (Nitro group)	Knot
1	Sun (by minor system)
246	Nourish (by phonetic)

Imagination: You are going to the picnic in a **hole(OH)** on the **sun (1)** and tying the **knots (NO_2)** to your friends to **nourish (246)** your friendship.

6. Benzyl Alcohol

Substitution

Benzyl Alcohol	Benezeer Bhutto (former Prime Minister of Pakistan) drinking alcohol
CH_2OH (Methyl Alcohol)	Methai*(Sweets) and alcohol

Imagination: **Benzeer Bhotto*** is drinking **alcohol** with **methai***(CH_2OH).

7. Methyl Salicylate

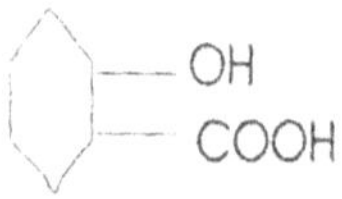

Substitutes

Methyl Salicylate	Methai* (sweets) Slices
OH	Hole
COOH	Hook
23	Name (by phonetic)

Imagination: You are making a **hole OH)** in **methai slices** with **a hook (COOH)** to write your **name (23)** there.

Note: Hole comes first in your imagination so OH will come in second position; hook comes next in the imagination so HOOC comes in the next i.e. third position.

8. Cinnamic Acid

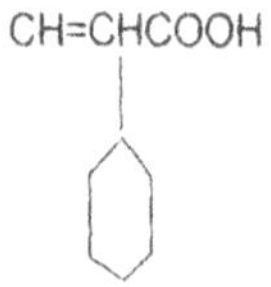

Substitutes

Cinnamic	Cinema
CH=CH COOH	CHaCHa-Hook

Imagine: In **cinema** hall, your **chacha (CH=CH)** is holding a **hook (COOH)** and is trying to pull out of screen the characters of the movie.

9. Styrene

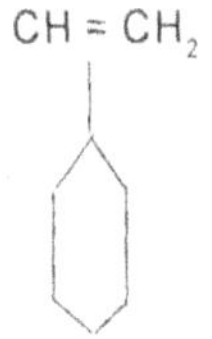

Substitutes:-

Styrene	Stereo
$CH=CH_2$	CHaCHa-shoe(2=shoe, by minor system)

Here we have substituted 2 for shoe by minor system.

Imagination: On **stereo** music your **chacha (CH=CH)** is dancing wearing **shoes (2)** only.

10. Furan

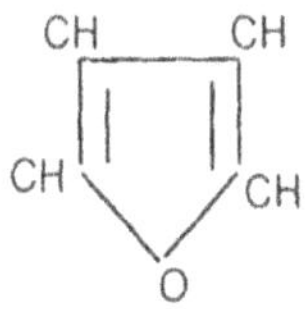

Substitutes

Furan	Kuran*(a holy book)

We can associate this pentagon to five times namaz. We can associate the upper part to a mat and 'O' to an agarbatti* stand.

CH- CH	CHaCHa
CH-CH	CHaCHa
O	Agarbatti *(incense stick) stand

Imagination: Your **CHaCHaji** reads **Kuran*(Furan) five times (five corners)** a day sitting on a mat and lighting an **agarbatti (O)** in front of him.

In the similar manner, we can make our own associations for

other structure formulae. The associations can be manipulated in several ways using creativity.

We should revise the funny associations to give them a permanent space in our memory. Revising the structural formulae with the help of such abnormal associations makes the revision interesting, refreshing and efficient. Such funny associations save our revision time once they are formed and boost up our confidence since we remember them for longer.

CHAPTER -17

NAME REACTIONS

Reactions can also be memorised by applying the same rules. What we are required to do is -simply convert the radicals taking part in the reaction into visual substitutes and then associating them by making a funny story. In case of name reactions, name of the reaction is also included in the story. Mostly story is started with the name of the reaction which makes us recall the entire equation. Logic is simple -as we see the name of the reaction we shall automatically be reminded of the equation instantly. Here some equations are taken as examples.

1) REIMER AND TIEMANN'S REACTION

a) 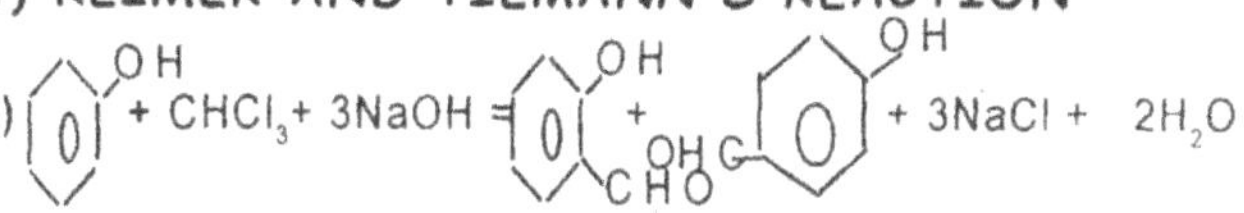

Phenol Chloroform Caustic soda Salicylaldehyde Para isomer

b) 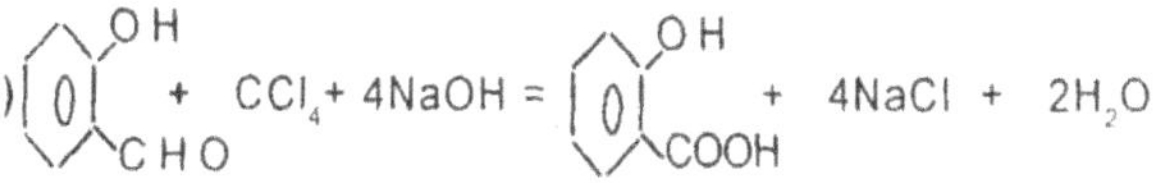

Phenol carbon tetra chloride Salicylic Acid

Reaction 'a' could be substituted like this-

a) Substitution

Phenol	Phenol bottle
Reimar Tiemann	Rima Sen* (actress) and a tie wearing man.
$CHCl_3$ (Chloroform)	Fainting down (you can use fainting as a symbol of chloroform)
NaOH(Caustic Soda)	Soap (you can use soap as a symbol of caustic soda)
Salicyaldehyde	Slicing of head
Isomer	Same looking man i.e. clone

NaCl	Common salt (NaCl is known as common salt)
H_2O	Water

Substituted form (a)

Phenol+ A man is fainting +Caustic soda=Slicing of head+Same clone emerged + Salt + Water

Imagination (a):

Rima Sen and a **tie-wearing man** are standing. Rima makes him drink **phenol** and he **faints down**. Rima washes him with **soap**. She makes **slices of the head** of tie man but from his blood a **clone** is formed. Rima throws **salt (NaCl)** on the clone and he melts down into **water.**

b) Substitution

CCl_4(Carbon tetra chloride)	Car-four-clown i.e. four clowns in a car.
Salicylic Acid	Sali*(sister-in-law) on cycle

Substituted form (b)

Phenol + Four clowns in a car + Soap= Sali* on cycle + Salt +Water

Imagination (b):

Rima Sen gives **phenol** to **four clowns sitting in a car** to drink. As they drink it **soap bubbles** start coming out of their mouth. Suddenly their **sali* on cycle** comes there and helps them by giving **salt** and **water.**

2. GATTERMANN-KOCH ALDEHYDE SYNTHESIS

$$C_6H_6 + Cl.CHO \xrightarrow{\text{anhyd } AlCl_3} C_6H_5CHO + HCl$$

Benzene Chloroaldehyde Benzaldehyde

In this reaction if we separate HCl then C_6H_5CHO obviously is the second product.

So we'll make association between C_6H_6, Cl.CHO, catalyst anhyd $AlCl_3$ and HCl and we'll leave C_6H_5CHO in our association since we can logically recollect it.

Substitution

Gattermann	Gutter man
C_6H_6	Benezeer Bhutto(former Prime Minister of Pakistan)
Cl.CHO	Clown-hide i.e.Clown is hiding
Anhydrous	Dry
$AlCl_3$	Aluminum-clown i.e.Clown with alloo*.
HCl(Hydrochloric acid)	HCL Company

Substituted form

Benezeer+Hiding clown =---- ----+ HCL Company

Imagination:

A **gutter man** has attacked **Benezeer Bhutto**. Seeing this **clown hides** himself in the gutter and throws **alloo*** from there on gutter man which falls in the **HCL company**.

3)SCHMIDT REACTION

R-COOH	+ N_3H	=	R-NH_2	+	Co_2+ N_2
Acid	**Hydrazoic acid**		**Primary Amine**		

Substitution

Schmidt	Chemist
R-COOH	Hook
Hydrazoic Acid	Hydra and jonk*(Leech)
Amine	Mine
CO_2	Black air
N_2	Gentleman at night

Substituted form

Hook + Hydra and jonk* = Mine + Black air +Gentleman at night

Imagination: A **chemist** is catching **hydra and jonk** with a big hook and putting them into a **mine**. In the mine **black air** is filled. At **night a gentleman** comes and pulls them out of the mine.

CHAPTER- 22

PREFERENTIAL SERIES

Functional group	Name
-COOH	Carboxylic Acids
$-SO_3H$	Sulphonic Acids
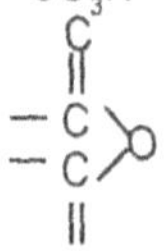	Acid Anhydrides
-COOR	Esters
-COCl	Acid Chloride
$-CONH_2$	Amides
$C \equiv N$	Cyanides
$-N \equiv C$	Isocyanides
-CHO	Aldehydes
>CO	Ketons
-OH	Alcohols
-SH	Thioalcohols
$-NH_2$	Amides
-OR	Ether
C =C	Alkenes
$C \equiv C$	Alkynes
-X	Halogens
$-NO_2$	Nitro

Substitution

Carboxylic Acids	A boxer in a car
Sulphonic Acids	Cell phone
Acid Anhydrides	Acid dried up
Esters	Easter festival
Acid Chloride	Clown ride
Amides	In the mid
Cyanides	Cyanide poison
Isocyanides	Ice for cyanide
Aldehydes	All hide
Ketons	Kite

Alcohols	Alcohol bottles
Thioalcohols	Alcohol in a thal*(big plate)
Amines	In a mine
Ethers	Thar Desert
Alkenes	Keys
Alkynes	Kai*(algae)
Halogens	Hello saying gentlemen
Nitro	Knot

Mental movie

A **boxer** is sitting in a car talking on his **cell phone.** Suddenly his phone breaks down as the **acid** in the cell **dries up**. To bring the acid he goes to a shop where everybody is busy in celebrating the **Easter festival.** When he asks for acid a **clown rides** up on a high escalator to bring the acid .But as he reaches the **mid** of the escalator he starts fainting down as he smells **cyanide** there. Boxer feeds him with a lot of **ice** to nullify the affect of the **cyanide.** The clown is very happy after gaining consciousness and he gives **all** the **hidden kites** to the boxer as a reward. The boxer comes into an open field to fly the kites. As the kites strike the sky it starts raining. But what is this! **Alcohol bottles** are falling in rain instead of water. After collecting the **alcohol bottles** in a **big thal*** he enters **a mine** to store them. But, he finds that there is **Thar Desert** in the mine.The boxer puts his bottles there locks them and walks out of the Thar Desert swinging the **keys.** Oh! He slips down on the way due to **kai*.** Seeing this some **gentlemen** run towards him to help him and say, "**Hello**". Now, you tie **knots** in the hands of the gentlemen for the friendship.

TEST

1. See if you can write the preferential series in the given order.

....

....

....

....

....

....

....

....

....

....

....

....

....

....

....

....

....

....

....

....

....

Time taken............

Score ....

QUICK RECALL TECHNIQUES FOR FORMULAE

CHAPTER -23

MATH'S FORMULAE

Mathematics and physics are logical subjects. There is not much memorisation part. We need to understand a problem and then give it a solution. To solve the problems we need to remember formulae and mostly students commit formulae to their mind by rote. If we don't revise the formulae for some days we are likely to confuse in them easily. We know we cannot solve a problem on forgetting the formula even if we know the mechanism to solve it.

In the context of forgetting the formulae, I would like to throw some light on the types of forgetting.

1) It may be partial forgetting or confusion.

2) It may be total forgetting.

1) In case of partial forgetting or confusion

To forget formula partially means that we are not able to recollect a certain part of the formula otherwise we can write the formula.

Example $\quad \sin 3A = 3\sin A - 4\sin^3 A$

$\cos 3A = 4\cos^3 A - 3\cos A$

In the two formula given above the opposite sequence is followed i.e. for the formula Sin3A, it is started with 3Sin A and for the formula cos 3A, it gets started with $4\cos^3 A$.

If we are able to remove the confusion in one formula and are able to write it down correctly, we can easily recall the second formula because it is just reverse of the previous one.

Now, we shall highlight the **area of forgetting or confusion** in the first formula.

$\underline{\sin 3A = 3\sin A} - 4\sin^3 A$

We can associate the two sides by visualising them with the help of substitution.

Substitution

Sin	Sen (Sushmita Sen)
3	Tree (by minor system)
A	Apple

Substituted form

Sen. tree . apple= tree. sen. apple --4Sin^3 A

Imagination: Sushmita Sen climbs up a tree to pluck apples (Sin 3A) but she gets trapped between the tree and apples (3SinA)

Now,confusion in the formula Sin 3A is eliminated.Whenever we are likely to be confused in the formula ,our imagination that Sen is trapped between the apples and the tree will save us. Since second formula i.e. Cos3A, is following the reverse order so its confusion is automatically removed.

Example 2

Some times we are confused in the names of the shapes. If we are confused in the names, we are likely to put wrong formula and hence are likely to make mistake.

Here is an example -

Segment  Sector 

Student may confuse whether a particular figure is segment on sector. If we link the name with the shape, we can remove the confusion.

In the first case we can link the shape to a bowl. Segment can be thought as mint leaves. We can think that 'mint leaves' are lying in a 'bowl'.It will remind us that segment is bowl shaped figure.

Confusion about the name of the remaining shape is automatically removed but if we are interested in linking this also we can link the second figure with a piece of cake and we can substitute sector as 'Victor'.Now, we can make association between the two by thinking that uncle 'Victor' likes 'cake' very much.

2) In case of total forgetting

a)Recollection by logics

b)Registration through creativity

a) Recollection by logics

Logical method to recollect a forgotten formula is well known. In this method we try to write down a particular formula by thinking about it logically. *For example-*

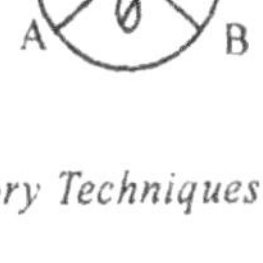

Area of sector of a circle= $\frac{\pi R^2 \theta}{360^0}$

If we forget this formula we should try to recall it as

- Sector is OAB
- The formula for the area of entire Circle is πr^2.
- The central angle of circle is 360^0 and the angle of sector is θ
- So area of sector will be $\frac{\pi R^2 \theta}{360^0}$

b)Registration through creativity

When we forget a formula frequently and also not able to get the formula logically ,we should apply some creativity on the entire formula to feed it into our permanent memory.

For example:

$$\tan 3\theta = \frac{3 \tan\theta - \tan^3\theta}{1 - 3\tan^2\theta}$$

Substitution

tan	tin
3	tree
θ (theta)	threatening
1	Sun
2	Shoe

We can convert the formula into symbols as -

tin- tree -threatening=Tree.Tin-Tin^{Tree}/Sun-TreeTin^{Shoe}

Imagination: We can imagine that a tree is threatening to a tin. To threaten first tree beats the tin from back side (3 tanθ) than from above **(tan3θ)**.Sun (1)comes down**(divided sign)** and makes tree and tin stand before him and asks the reason for violence and comes to know tin was actually guilty.Then sun also beats tree with shoe **(3 tan^2 θ)**. Since threatening is a negative process so we'll put negative sign up and down.

We will not take much time to recall the formula as we will imagine the entire happening very fast. This is because we can imagine at a greater speed than thinking or writing.

Some Hits For Substitution

Here is a list of substitutes for trigonometrical and other mathematical terms. We can use them to retain the formulae and can also create our own substitutes if we like.

Terms	Substitutes
Sin	Sen (Sushmita Sen)
Cos	Cosco ball
Tan	Tin
Cot	Coat
Secant	Cent bottle
Cosecant	Koi Sikh i.e. a Sikh (Sardarji)
+	Doctors Sign
—	Not good ,something bad
(Under root)	Umbrella
A	Apple
B	Ball etc.

Although the formulae taken in this chapter may not confuse you but many other students get confused in these formulae.

Here the purpose is to create awareness about the techniques for clearing confusion or retaining the entire formula.

Area of confusion and retention of formulae may vary from student to student. A formula which is always forgettable to one student may be very much clear to another student .One student may always be confused in particular formula another may never be confused in that.

So we should find our own list of formulae which we need to retain through creativity. As I earlier said that mathematics is a subject of practice and practice. During the practice we should pay attention to the formulae which we frequently forget, note them down, practice creativity on them and retain them. Though only math's formulae have been discussed here but the same principles can be applied to physics formulae with equal efficiency.

CHAPTER-24

PHYSICS FORMULAE

Coding in visual images is particularly useful in memorising physics formulae as well. We can arrange the terms in a formula to get some visual image.

For example1

Force on a current carrying conductor placed in a magnetic field.

$F = BLI \sin\theta$

After arranging the terms

$F = BIL \sin\theta$

Imagine: A **conductor (Bus conductor)** is carrying current in the **magnetic field** and **Sushmita Sen (sin θ)** is **forcing (F)** him to pay the **bill (BIL)** .

Example 2

De Broglie waves

$$\lambda = \frac{h}{m v}$$

After arranging the terms

$$\lambda mv = h$$

Imagine: A **dog is barking (De Brolie waves**) on a lamb (lambdaλ). Horrified lamb **moved (mv)** away to a **hospital (h)**.

CHAPTER-25

PREFIXES FOR EXPRESSING POWERS OF 10

Personalise the prefixes for expressing powers of 10 by applying imagination to them. Here are some memory aids to make them interesting, but the most effective memory aid are those that have personal meaning.Mnemonics are fun, and the time spent finding or making up your own will help to imprint them in your memory.

Power of 10	Prefix
10^{24}	Yotta
10^{21}	Zetta
10^{18}	Exa
10^{15}	Peta
10^{12}	Tera
10^{9}	Giga

Power of 10 **Prefix**
10^{24} Yotta

Original **Substitute**
24 Nari (by phonetic)
Yotta Yotha* (a fighter)

Imagine: A **yotha*(a fighter)** is fighting for a beautiful **nari*(24)**.

Power of 10 **Prefix**
10^{21} Zotta

Original **Substitute**
21 Net (by phonetic)
Zetta Jet

Imagine: You are trying to catch **jet (zetta)** aero plane with a big **net (21)**.

Power of 10 **Prefix**
10^{18} Exa

Original **Substitute**
18 Specs (by minor system)

Exa	Example

Imagine: Your new brand **specs (18)** are **exemplary (exa)**.

Power of 10	**Prefix**
10^{15}	Peta

Original	**Substitute**
15	Hook (by minor system)
Peta	Pet

Imagine: You are tying your **pet (peta)** with a **hook (15).**

Power of 10	**Prefix**
10^{12}	Tera

Original	**Substitute**
12	Duck (by minor system)
Tera	Teer*(arrow)

Imagine: You are hitting a **teer* (tera)** to a **duck (12).**

Power of 10	**Prefix**
10^{9}	Giga

Original	**Substitute**
9	Wine (by minor system)
Giga	Jija* (brother in law)

Imagine: Jija (giga) is drinking **wine (9).**

MNEMONICS FOR MEMORISING BIOLOGY

CHAPTER-26

BIOLOGICAL TERMINOLOGY

Bringing imagination to any subject helps to commit it to memory. We can make boring information interesting by mentally colouring it. As we have discussed earlier a strong memory depends on our ability to link new information with data already stored in our brains, thus giving it a frame of reference in much the same way that a detective pieces together clues.

In this chapter, we shall learn how to code biological terminology into more memorable words, phrases or sentences.

For example

Kalology is related to the study of human beauty. As we read this term, we can make a link between the two by thinking that a Kala* (black) person is studying beautiful human faces.

Study of fungi is known as mycology. We can connect them by visualising that in the college we study nothing but have fun.

The name of the smallest fish is pandaka. We can remember the name of fish by thinking that we are playing with a very small fish. It is so small that we can cover (daka*) it with our pen (pan)

CHAPTER - 27

THE GENETIC CODES

	U		C		A		G		
U	UUU	Phenyla lanine	UCU	Serine	UAU	Tyrosine	UGU	Cysteine	U
	UUC		UCC		UAC		UGC		C
	UUA	Leucine	UCA		UAA	Stop	UGA	Stop	A
	UUG		UCG		UAG	Stop	UGG	Tryptophan	G
C	CUU	Leucine	CCU	Proline	CAU	Histidine	CGU	Arginine	U
	CUC		CCC		CAC		CGC		C
	CUA		CCA		CAA	Glutamine	CGA		A
	CUG		CCG		CAG		CGG		G
A	AUU	Isoleucine	ACU	Threonine	AAU	Asparagine	AGU	Serine	U
	AUC		ACC		AAC		AGC		C
	AUA	Methionine,	ACA		AAA	Lysine	AGA	Arginine	A
	AUG	Staart	ACG		AAG		AGG		G
G	GUU	Valine	GCU	Alanine	GAU	Aspartate	GGU	Glycine	U
	GUC		GCC		GAC		GGC		C
	GUA		GCA		GAA	Glutamate	GGA		A
	GUG		GCG		GAG		GGG		G

To memorise this table through mnemonics we shall have to examine the table thoroughly. After examining we find one thing common in the table that first two letters are followed by the letters U.C.A and G respectively in each subcolumn. So, in each subcolumn when we'll memorise the codons along with their special name, we shall leave the last letter and only pay attention to the first two letters.

We have no difficulty in remembering that each subcolumn contains four codons and in each subcolumn the first two letters of each codon are similar. For example-for the first subcolumn it is UU, for the second subscolumn it is CU for the third sub column it is AU and so on.

Leaving the exceptional case that exists in the **third** and **thirteenth** sub column, we find here a general trend that if two amino acids are there in a subcolumn then first two codons are linked with the first amino acid and remaining last two codons are linked with the second amino acid. For example: in first subcolumn UUU and UUC are associated with phenylalanine and last two codons UUA and UUG are associated with Leucine.

When one amino acid is there in a subcolumn then it is associated with all the four codons.

In case you find three amino acids in a subcolumn **(see subcolumn 13)** then first two codons will be associated to first amino acid , third codon to second amino acid and forth codon to third amino acid.We can remember this by thinking that first amino acid is being favoured so it get two codons and remaining two codons are being distributed equally between the remaining two amino acids.

Note: Third subcolumn is an exceptional case where there are two amino acids and first amino acid is associated with first three codons and next amino acid is associated with the last remaining codon.

Now we start memorising the table for genetic codes-

Subcolumn1

UUU	
UUC	Phenylalanine
UUA	Leucine
UUG	

After removing the last letter from the codons, subcolumn will look like-

UU	
UU	Phenylalanine
UU	Leucine
UU	

Substitution

UU	YoYo (YoYo is a toy)
Phenylalanine	Phenol bottle and Lenin*(a

	Philosopher)
Leucine	Lucy* (Lucy Grey is a character in poems)

Imagination: Sitting on a **YoYo(UU) Lenin** is holding a **phenol (Phenylalanine)** bottle and giving it to drink to **Lucy (Leucine).**

Note: Here the first amino acid is linked with first two codons and second amino acid is linked with the last two codons.

Subcolumn 2

CUU	
CUC	Leucine
CUA	
CUG	

After eliminating the last letter-

CU	
CU	Leucine
CU	
CU	

Substitution

CU	See you
Leucine	Lucy Grey*

Imagination: Lucy Grey is **seeing you** off.

Subcolumn3

AUU	
AUC	Isoleucine
AUA	
AUG	Methionine, start

After removing the last letter

AU	
AU	Isoleucine
AU	
AU	Methionine

Substitution

AU	Gold (As Au is the symbol for gold in chemistry)

Isoleucine	Ice-Lucy* i.e. ice and Lucy Grey
Methionine	Methai*(Sweets) Start

Imagination: Lucy is eating **ice (isoleucine)**-and **methai*** in a **gold (AU)** cone.

Note: Since Lucy likes ice too much so major number of codons i.e. first three codons are associated with ice and remaining last i.e. fourth with methai*

Subcolumn 4

GUU
GUC — Valine
GUA
GUG

After separating the last letter-

GU
GU — Valine
GU
GU

Substitution

GU	Gun
Valine	Wall

Imagination: Visualise a **Gun** is lying against a big **wall.**

Subcolumn 5

UCU
UCC — Serine
UCA
UCG

After removing the last letter

UC
UC — Serine
UC
UC

Substitution

UC	USE (Give attention to the sound)
Serine	Shrine (A holy place where people go to pray to fulfill their desires)

Imagination: People **use (UC) shrines (Serine)** to **fulfill** their wishes.

Subcolumn 6

CCU	
CCC	Proline
CCA	
CCG	

After removing the last letter

CC	
CC	Proline
CC	
CC	

Substitution

CC	Shishi* (a small bottle)
Proline	Pari*(an angel) in a line

Imagination: A **Pari** is standing in a **line (proline)** holding a **shishi* (CC).**

Subcolumn 7

ACU	
ACC	Threonine
ACA	
ACG	

Eliminating the last letter

AC	
AC	Threonine
AC	
AC	

Substitution

AC	AC (Air Conditioners)
Threonine	Throw

Imagination: Your **AC** is not cooling the room so you are **throwing (threonine)** it out.

Subcolumn 8

GCU	
GCC	Alanine
GCA	
GCG	

Removing the last letter

GC	
GC	Alanine
GC	
GC	

Substitution

GC	Jassi*(TV Serial character)
Alanine	Lenin* (Philosopher)

Imagination: **Jassi (GC)** is meeting with **Lenin (Alanine)**

Subcolumn 9

UAU	
UAC	Tyrosine
UAA	Stop
UAG	Stop

After separating last letter

UA	
UA	Tyrosine
UA	
UA	Stop

Substitution

UA	UAE
Tyrosine	Tyre-Sen*(Sushmita Sen)
Stop	Stop
Stop	Stop

Imagination: Sitting on a **tyre Sen** is going to **UAE**. People are **stopping** her saying,"You can not reach there on tyre; stop, stop".

Subcolumn 10

CAU	
CAC	Histidine
CAA	Glutamine
CAG	

Removing the last letter

CA	
CA	Histidine
CA	
CA	Glutamine

Substitution

CA	CA (Chartered Accountant)
Histidine	Hysteria
Glutamine	Looting-mine

Imagination: Whenever a **CA** gets **hysteria (histidine)** attacks people take him to a **mine** for **looting (glutamine)** him.

Subcolumn 11

AAU	
AAC	Asparagine
AAA	Lysine
AAG	

After separating the last letter

AA	
AA	Asparagine
AA	Lysine
AA	

Substitution

AA	Aaa..aa.. (sound of pain)
Asparagine	Casper (mosquito repellent)
Lysine	Lice

Imagination: You are crying with pain **aa..aa**.. as your **Casper mosquito repellent** is emitting **lice** which are biting you.

Subcolumn 12

GAU	
GAC	Aspartate
GAA	Glutamate
GAG	

After eliminating the last letter

GA	
GA	Aspartate
GA	Glutamate
GA	

Substitution

GA	GAna
Aspartate	Expert
Glutamate	Loot-Mate

Imagination: An **expert (aspartate)** is **looting** your **mate** (**glutamate**) by singing a **gana* (GA)**.

Subcolumn 13.

UGU	
UGC	Cysteine
UGA	Stop
UGG	Tryptophan

After eliminating the last letter

UG	
UG	Cysteine
UG	Stop
UG	Tryptophan

Substitution

UG	UGC (University Grant Commission)
Cysteine	Crystal
Stop	Stop

Tryptophan Try

Imagination: UGC is gifting precious **crystals (cysteine)** to the students who have **stopped trying** for UCG exams as it does not want any headache for arranging exams.

Subcolumn 14

CGU	
CGC	Arginine
CGA	
CGG	

Eliminating the last letter

CG	
CG	Arginine
CG	
CG	

Substitution

CG	Sage
Arginine	Archie's greeting cards

Imagination: A **sage (CG)** is distributing the **archie's greeting cards (arginine)** among the people to inculcate love.

Subcolumn 15

AGU	
AGC	Serine
AGA	Arginine
AGG	

After removing the last letter

AG	
AG	Serine
AG	Arginine
AG	

Substitution

Ag	Aged people
Serine	Shrine

Arginine	Archie's greeting cards

Imagination: Old **aged** people are going to a **shrine (serine)** taking **archie's greeting cards (arginine)** for the God.

Subcolumn 16

GGU	
GGC	Glycine
GGA	
GGG	

After removing the last letter

GG	
GG	Glycine
GG	
GG	

Substitution

GG	Jija ji
Glycine	Glass

Imagination: Your **Jija ji (CG)** is seeing himself in a **glass (glycine).**

You have to revise these associations to be able to give a prompt response. For example - If you are asked

UUU
UUC
UUA
UUG

belong to which amino acids, answer would automatically come to your mind phenylalanine and leucine and so on.

CHAPTER -28

DIAGRAM

Whenever we are required to learn a new diagram we should see it carefully and try to associate its shape with something familiar. Some times, we can link its shape with the actual things as has been done in the example given in this chapter.The human brain has been compared to human brain itself. But, it has to be seen very big, so big that we can enter the brain and see what activities are going on there. Also we are free to link the figure with something else we know. For example, in case of plant cell we can compare the diagram to a field.

After comparing the diagram all the naming of the various parts of the diagram should be read carefully before their substitutes are made. After deciding where to start from we should do numbering as we have done in the case of human brain diagram.

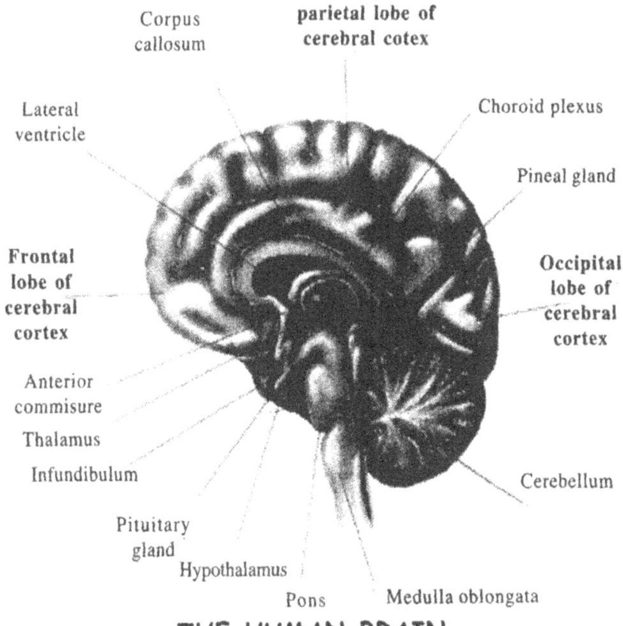

THE HUMAN BRAIN

Substitution

Substitutes we have taken for the diagram are given below-

1. Medulla oblongata-Models in a long gate
2. Pons- Ponds* (a company)
3. Hypothalamus- Hippopotamus
4. Pituitary gland - Pit
5. Infundibulum - In fun
6. Thalamus - Thal* (plate)
7. Anterior commissure - Aunt with commissioner
8. Frontal lobe of cerebral cortex - Front lobby
9. Lateral ventricle - Late van
10. Corpus callosum - Corps call
11. Parietal lobe of cerebral cortex - Parents in lobby
12. Choroid plexus - Cord-lux* (a soap)
13. Pineal gland - Pin
14. Occipital lobe of cerebral cortex- Hospital lobby
15. Cerebellum - Celebrating

Imagination: In our **brain** there is a **long gate** and **models** are entering the brain through the gate **(modulla oblongata).** Now, they start modeling for the products of **ponds company (pons)**. A **hippopotamus (hypothalamus)** sitting in a **pit (pituitary gland)** is enjoying the show-and saying loudly," I am **in fun (infundibulum)**". Suddenly, he stops saying this because he sees someone coming towards him taking a big **thal* (thalamus).** As the person approaches him he finds that it is his **aunt** who is coming along with a **commissioner (anterior commissure)**. See the aunt taking him to the **front lobby (frontal lobe of cerebral cortex)**. They want to go out so they are waiting for a Van. The **van** comes **late (lateral ventricle)**. As they sit in the van they **call** army **corps (corpus callosum)** to protect themselves as they are going out. They see instead of army corps their **parents'** are coming to **lobby (parietal lobe of cerebral cortex)** holding a **lux soap** tied with a **cord (choroids plexus)** which they are tossing up and down. To stop them from doing this they cut the cord with a **big pin (pineal gland)**. Parents' start crying due to this so they take them to a **hospital lobby (occipital lobe of cerebral cortex)**. But, they find that all people in hospital are **celebrating (cerebellum)** and no one is working.

We should revise these interesting associations in our mind emphasising the main words which we aim to remember. We should list the diagrams which are difficult to remember, then we should associate the figure and its naming with something familiar. After some practice we shall enjoy this like a game.

TEST

Mention the naming.

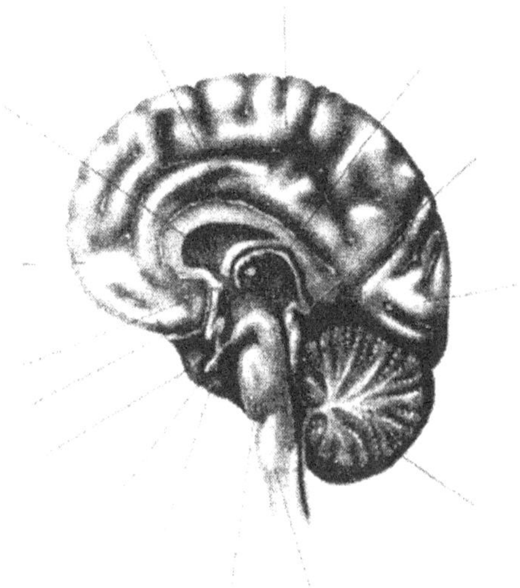

Time taken.........
Score.........

Ultrastructure of a plant cell

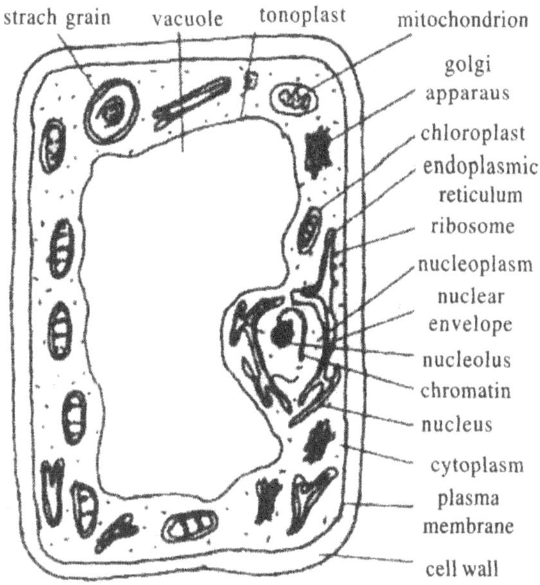

The immediate thing which may strike in our mind while looking at the diagram could be a mental picture of a big ground surrounded by walls at all the four sides with a swimming pool.

Now, look at the naming starting from the word 'starch grain' and link them with the visual words which come into our mind.

Original	**Substitute**
Starch grain	Torch
Vacuole	Vacuum
Tonoplast	Tin and plastic
Mitochondrion	Meeting and cone
Golgi apparatus	Gol* (round) apparatus
Chloroplast	Coloured plastic
Endoplasmic	End -plus(sign)
Reticulum	Rat
Ribosome	Some-ribbon
Nucleoplasm	Nakli*(imitation) plastic

Nuclear envelope	Nuclear furnace and envelope
Nucleolus	Necklace
Chromatin	Crow and mat
Nucleus	New-class
Cytoplasm	Seat
Plasma membrane	Member holding plus (sign)
Cell wall	Wall made up of cells

We can memorise the diagram easily by fabricating a funny and interesting story by joining all the words together.

We can make memorisation of biological diagram fun by comparing its shape with some similar looking picture and then linking its naming with a ridiculous or logical story.

CHAPTER -29

MULTIPLE CHOICE QUESTIONS BOTANY

1) Which of the following is a spherical shaped bacterium?

(a) Bacillus (b) *Coccus*

(c) Spirillum (d) Vibrio

Substitutes

Coccus - Cock

Bacterium - Bacteria

Imagine: Cock is attacking on **spherical shaped bacteria**.

2) Escherichia coli occurs in

(a) Milk (b) Water

(c) Soil (d) *Intestine of man*

Substitute

Escherichia - Cherry coloured chiria* (bird)

Imagine: In the intestine of a man a **cherry coloured chiria*** is found.

3) Who discovered transduction in bacteria?

(a) Wollman and Jocob (b) Laderberg and Tatum

(c) *Zinder and Laderberg* (d) Herelle and Twort

Substitute

Zinder & Laderberg - Zin*(ghost) on a ladder

Imagine: Zin*(zinder) on a **ladder (laderberg)** is observing **transduction in bacteria**.

4) **Photoautotrophic bacteria contain the pigment**

(a) Chlorophyll (b) *Bacteriocholophyll*

(c) Carotene (d) No pigment

Substitutes

Photoautotrophic - Photo of trophy

Bacteriocholophyll - Coloured bacteria

Imagine: You are taking **photo** of a **trophy** which is **pigmented** due to **colourful bacteria**.

5) **Which of the following is an autotrophic bacterium?**

(a) *Nitrobacter* (b) Clostridium

(c) Rhizobium (d) Azotobacter

Substitutes

Nitrobacter - Bacteria in the night

Autotrophic - Trophy

Imagine: At **night,** all **bacteria** get converted into a **trophy** shape.

6) **Salmonella typhosa causes**

(a) Typhoid (b) Paratyphoid

(c) Whooping cough (d) Pneumonia

Substitute

Salmonella - Salman Khan*(actor)

Imagine: Salman is suffering from **typhoid** so he is not coming to the shooting.

7) **Triple antigen is**

(a) Vaccine against Polio, Rabies and Hepatitis

(b) A vaccine against Malaria, Typhoid and Cancer

(c) A vaccine against Tetanus, Whooping Cough and Diphtheria

(d) Mixture of Viruses that causes Tetanus, Diphtheria and Whooping cough

Substitutes

Triple - Three

Antigen - Aunt sitting in a Zen car

Imagine: Three aunts sitting in a Zen car are giving **vaccines** against **tetanus, whooping cough and diphtheria** to the children.

8) Heterocysts are found in

a) *Nosto* (b) Blue-green algae

(c) Seed bearing plants (d) None of these

Substitutes

Heterocysts - Heater

Nosto - Not in stock

Imagine: Heater is **not** found **in the stock**.

9) Red tide in sea is caused by

(a) Red algae (b) *Diatoms*

(c) Dinophyceae (d) Phaeophyceae

Substitute

Diatoms - Two atom bombs

Imagine: Tide in **sea** becomes red in colour when you throw **two atom bombs** into it.

10) Diatoms are also known as

(a) Cyanobacteria (b) Blue-green algae

(c) Green algae *(d) Golden brown algae*

Substitutes

Diatoms - Two atom bombs

Golden brown algae - Golden brown algae

Imagine: Visualise **two atom bombs** are covered with **golden brown algae**.

11) The fruiting structure in cellular slime moulds is known as

(a) Pseudocarp	*(b) Sporocarp*
(c) Sporangium	(d) Sporogonium

Substitutes

Sporocarp	-	Sparrow in a car
Slime	-	Slim

Imagine: A **sparrow in a car** is talking on a **slim cell phone** and enjoying eating a **fruit**.

12) Cellular slime moulds are

(a) Haploid	(b) Diploid
(c) Triploid	(d) Polyploid

Substitutes

Cellular	-	Cell phone
Slime	-	Slim
Haploid	-	Help

Imagine: A **slim cell phone helps** you a lot in giving you a style.

CHAPTER -30

MULTIPLE CHOICE QUESTIONS ZOOLOGY

1 **What is the most important factor for the success of animal population?**

(a) Natality (b) Unlimited food
(c) Adaptability (d) Inter-species activity.

Substitutes

Adaptability - Adopting

Imagine: Visualise animals are **adopting baby** animals and hence increasing their **population**.

2 **In coming years, skin related disorders will be more common due to**

(a) Pollution in the air.
(b) Use of detergents.
(c) Water pollution.
(d) Depletion of ozone layer.

Substitutes

Depletion - deep lotion
Ozone - Zone

Imagine: Visualise a girl using a **deep lotion** to give shine to some of the **zones** of her skin, but skin is getting **disordered** because of it.

3. **Which one of the following animal is known as man of the forest?**

(a) Gibbon (b) Orangutan
(c) Gorilla (d) Chimpanzee.

Substitutes

Orangutan	-	Orange

Imagine: Visualise an **animal** looking like a **man** who is eating **oranges** in the forest.

4 **The most important characteristics of class Aves is**

(a) Homothermous animals.
(b) Tetra pod vertebrates.
(c) Bipedal vertebrates.
(d) Exoskeleton of feathers.

Substitutes

Class Aves	-	Class in evening
Exoskeleton	-	Skeleton on which an axe is hanging

Imagine: Visualise an **evening class** in which teacher is showing a **skeleton** on which **an axe is hanging** and this is the most **important characteristic** of the evening class.

5 **The head capsule of cockroach is formed by segments numbering**

(a) 4. (b) 5.
(c) 10. (d) 8.

Substitutes

Capsule	-	Capsule
8	-	Plate

Imagine: Visualise a **cockroach** holding a **plate** on its head in which **capsules** are lying.

6 **True Coelom is covered by**

(a) Ectoderm. (b) Endoderm.
(c) Mesoderm. (d) Ector and endoderm.

Substitutes

Coelom	-	Coal

Mesoderm - Mess and drum

Imagine: Visualise a **lot of coal** lying **in drum** in a **mess**.

7. **Oxygen liberated during photosynthesis comes from-**
   (a) Water
   (b) Co_2
   (c) Chlorophyll
   (d) Phosphoglyceric acid

Substitute

Oxygen - Ox

Imagine: Ox is taking **photo** of **water** scene.

8. **The main difference between chlorophyll a and b is that chlorophyll 'a'-**
   (a) Has methyl group whereas chlorophyll b has -CHO group
   (b) Is linear whereas chlorophyll b is branched
   (c) Has prophyrin and chlorophyll b has phytol tail
   (d) Is a more oxidized form

Substitutes

Chlorophyll	-	Colourful
Methyl	-	Methai*(sweets)
a	-	Apple
b	-	Ball
CHO (aldehyde group)	-	All hide

Imagine: You are eating a **colourful apple** which is sweet as **methai***and **hiding all** the **colourful balls** so that you can play with them alone.

9. **Calvin cycle-**
   (a) Depends on light
   (b) Does not depend on light
   (c) Occurs both in dark and light
   (a) None of the above

Substitutes

Calvin	-	Kelvinator refrigerator
Cycle	-	Cycle

Imagine: Visualise that you have bought a **Kelvinator refrigerator** that **does not depend on light**.

10.Kranz type of anatomy is found in the leaves of

(a) C3 Plants
(b) C4 plants
(c) Both C and C
(d) None of the above

Substitutes

Kranz	-	Karna* (Mahabharat character)
Anatomy	-	Tomy (dog)
C4	-	Car (4=r, by phonetic system)

Imagine: **Karna*** is taking his **Tomy** out in a **car**.

11.Pigment system II is concerned with

(a) Co_2 fixation
(b) Photolysis of water
(c) Liberation of energy
(d) Co_2 reduction

Substitutes

Pigment	-	Pigmentation
II	-	Shoe
Photolysis	-	Photo of water

Imagine: You are taking **photo of water** suddenly you fall down in it and your **shoes** get **pigmented.**

12.The core metal of chlorophyll is

(a) Copper (b) Nickel
(c) Magnesium (d) Iron

Substitutes

Chlorophyll	-	Colourful
Magnesium	-	Maggie

Imagine: Visualise that you are making **Maggie** in a **colourful metal** vessel.

GENERAL

CHAPTER-31

PROCRASTINATION

Procrastination exists in all human beings. We all are trapped by procrastination at one time or another. However, this is a major problem for us. This chapter is an attempt to deal with the type of "excessive postponing" that impedes student's academic performance.

What do we mean by procrastination?

In simple language, procrastination is "the deliberate act of excessive postponing."

Why do people procrastinate?

On the one hand, procrastination is a dealing device that offers protection from fear or anxiety. For example- A student procrastinates to math's homework because it causes anxiety as questions are too hard to solve. Past failure which reinforces a negative self image with self-condemnation, anxiety and embarrassment as end result also stops a student start.

On the other hand, procrastination is a bad habit. There are two causes. One of them is justifying behaviour caused by perfectionism inadequacy and fear of discomfort.

The perfectionist endlessly rewrites draft after draft, worriedly seeking that perfect essay, missing the deadline the student with feelings of inadequacy "know" that they are incompetent and therefore avoid the unpleasantness of having their skills put to the test. Fear of discomfort or failure often paralyses many students and keep them from doing what should be done.

What are the symptoms of procrastination?

"I will start this early morning", (as if now it is not the right time to start.)

"I have got to start soon" (there is still plenty of time.)

"I'm preparing for the quiz, I have completed my homework but the project" (At least I'm getting something done.)

"Hey! there is still time" (the moment of deadline is yet to come). Due to procrastination you try to remain optimistic.
There are many such examples.

What are the consequences of procrastination?

How much trouble your procrastination causes supremely depends on the price you have to pay for that behaviour. But, usually it has the same net results in all areas of one's life- wasted time, missed opportunities, poor performance and increased stress.

How to cure procrastination?

Procrastination can be cured, but it requires energy and commitment. Always remember, greater energy is required to start change than to sustain change.

Some tips to cure procrastination are given here-

Admit the Problem

The first step to cure the problem is to admit it. If you don't know that you are a procrastinator then there is no question of curing it.

To admit it first is to monitor your behaviour pattern. Answer this honestly-

How frequently do you make excuses for not starting a task?

Now, divide the page into two columns and write down all your excuses in first column, challenge your faulty reasoning and write down your realistic thoughts in the second column.

Here is an example:

Excuse	Realistic Thought
I don't feel like doing it.	If I wait for the right mood I might never do it.
Right now I am not perfect enough to start it.	Perfectionism is nothing more than an illusion.
I will start it early in the morning (but now it is not the right time)	Right now I'm having plenty of time and I may not get up in the early morning at the right time. Besides, I have other important work to do in the morning.

Auto Suggestion

Auto suggestions are the positive suggestions given to ourselves in order to improve efficiency.

Labeling yourself as dumb or lazy will not help. Belittling yourself will only serve to perpetuate the cycle of procrastination. Give yourself positive suggestions through self-motivating statements such as-

- "There is no time like the present"
- "Perfectionism is nothing more than an illusion that keeps me from doing what I have to do right now."
- "The sooner I finish this work, the sooner I can enjoy my favourite T.V. show."

Setting Clear Goals

First decide what do you want to accomplish and how you would do that? Be specific. Give yourself a deadline. Figure out a time table with realistic goals at each step. For a big project divide the task into smaller portions. Start with a smaller portion and accomplish it step by step.

Prioritise

Write down the task to be done to accomplish your ultimate goal. Now, arrange them in the order of their importance. The greater the importance or urgency, the higher is priority. Start at the top of the list each day and work your way today. If the last thing is not done today, put it at the top of the list for tomorrow, if it is still that important or urgent.

Committing to the Task

Write a contract stating the task and deadlines that you are vowing to meet. Sign it. If you can tell parents, friends or teachers about your plans that will be better. It is amazing how responsible one becomes when vocalising the terms of the contract.

Reward Yourself

When you achieve a task on your to do list in given time celebrate it no matter how small. 'DO IT NOW' attitude deserves a pat on the back. Move on to bigger and greater things.

CHAPTER- 32

NOTE-MAKING

Why take notes during the lecture?

Taking notes develops a sense of listing, allowing the reader to recognise main ideas and to understand the organisation of the material. The students who are habitual of taking notes during the lecture not only record significant facts but also record the lecture's emphasis and perspectives.

Notes taken during the lecture provide the clearest and best indication of what the student should encounter in the exams. Taking notes also improves understanding as it keeps student's attention focused on the lecture, which also leads to better concentration and retention. The students who take notes in the class are active participants rather than passive listeners or daydreamers.

Taking notes helps the student sort out important information by synthesising and beginning the actual learning process. The student actually makes the material of his own.

The notes thus taken will become an excellent study aid, an external memory device and an instrument of reviewing and recitation. This process leads to long-term learning.

Facilitating your note making

- Attend the class regularly.
- Arrive on time.
- Keep up with reading assignments.
- Organise your note making material ahead of time and come mentally prepared.

Rewrite your class notes

Notes must be arranged in some logical manner so that you can understand and use them. Notes which you have taken in the class should be rewritten in your own words so that they can be legible and complete.

In cases, where lecturer speaks too fast it become necessary to rewrite the class notes to complete them. You can take help of other classmates. Exchange your notes with theirs. Exchange notes regularly if it proves beneficial.

During the lecture leave large empty spaces for filling the information you missed. Use symbols that will help you remember what is missing.

See the instructor after the class

Take the notes with you and ask the lecturer what you missed. Ask questions.

These class notes will give you a very good direction on what to particularly read from the textbooks and how to effectively prepare your own notes.

SQ3 R

A study technique to prepare your own notes.

Although, at first glance it seems to be an intricate and time consuming process. However, it gets easier and faster with practice and ensures thorough learning that in consequence facilitates "relearning" when you review for the exams. Give it a try!

S= SURVEY

Determine the structure and organisation of the chapter. Why? If you give your mind a general frame work of main ideas and structure, you will enable yourself to comprehend and retain the details you will read later.

How? Look quickly over the following key parts of your textbook to see what it is all about and how it is organised.

- Title
- Front and back cover information
- About the author
- Date of publication
- Introduction or preface
- Glossary

Before you read any chapter, look at the

- Title
- Introduction
- Headings & subheadings
- First sentence or bold lines of each paragraph
- Any diagrams, graphs etc.
- Conclusion or summaries

Then answer what is this all about?

Q=QUESTION

Convert each heading and sub-heading into a question. Especially, while you are practicing this technique write down the question.

Why? Because it will make you an active reader. Being an active reader will help you in understanding the material, combating boredom and will increase retention.

How?

- Set realistic time goals and number of pages to be read.
- Divide your chapter into small (1/2 page or 1 page as you like) sections. Then seek its answer. It will define the purpose of your reading.
- Try converting the subheading or first sentence into a question, using "who", "what", "when" and "how" if necessary. It will give you a focal point for crystallising a series of ideas.

R1 = READ

Now read only that section, which you have selected, looking for the answers of questions. Move quickly, sort out ideas and evaluate them.

Always remember: this time you are looking for something rather than simply looking at words. If contents do not relate to the question, give it only a glance. So read selectively.

Reading Tips

- Do not pick a chair that is too comfortable.
- Instead sit at a desk with a chair having straight back. That place should have plenty of light.
- Take breaks when you feel exhausted.
- After a short break you can return to your reading.
- If you are falling asleep while you read try reading aloud.

R2 = RECITE

Answer the questions in your own words, not the author's. Keep the answers brief. Then write the answers using only keywords, listing etc. that are needed to recall the entire idea. Follow the above technique for each section of the chapter.

R3 = REVIEW

Increase retention and cut cramming time up to 90% by the means of immediate and delayed review. Why? Because 40-50% of the material we read is forgotten very shortly (about 15 min.) after we read it. Immediate recall is an essential first step towards continued retention of the material.

How? Recall mentally or recite orally the highlights of what you have written. Ask yourself questions (may be the same ones you used before you read the section) and then answer them in your own words. Recall the chapter along with a friend, as it is possible what you don't recall, he/she might recall it.

CHAPTER-33

REVISION PLAN

Generally, students spend 5-6 hours to study a particular subject. When they are confident about what they study they put it aside. After few days when they need the material they sit to revise it and during the revision they are confronted with the fact that they have forgotten most of the material . They take again 2-3 hours to revise and bring their memory level to 100%.

When to revise the material we study- is a question of vital importance. And students must know the fact that we start forgetting the information within 24 hours.

So, it is necessary to take first revision next day.You will not take much time to revise the chapter. It will take initially 30-35 minutes, as the distortion is not much

Second revision should be done within next three days. It will take around 30 minutes again.

Students are suggested to go for the third revision within next seven days. It will again take around 15 minutes.

One can say -if he goes on revising the same things, how will he be able to find time for other subjects?

Here we see the total time taken in revisions according to revision plan is one hour fifteen minutes. And if we revise the material after a considerable gap we will take around 2-3 hours or even more. So, by giving frequent revisions we actually save our time and energy.

CHAPTER- 34

THE ART OF READING SCIENCES

Why do we need to polish the art of reading science?

Readings in science contain a large number of facts and details of derivations. This kind of reading requires an overall understanding of information presented in order to process details.

Placement of main ideas and details is usually straight forward (headings and subheadings), but grasping of all the details can be awesome as information is dense.

Organisational pattern is usually "relationships", i.e. ideas and details building upon previous information. A solid background of the basics in the discipline is necessary for a student to understand and comprehend the information.

Terminology in the science is subject specific and must be understood to comprehend information presented. Often important terms are bold faced or italicised. A review of terminology before reading and memorising them through **LINK SYSTEM** increases understanding and comprehension.

Diagrams, figures, charts and graphs are numerous. Time is needed to study these as these visual aids help to integrate information and visualisation aids in the understanding and retention of information.

Knowledge and comprehension of the readings and lectures must be taken to an "application" level i.e. the ideas learned should be applied to new or different situation other than those presented in the texts or lectures. Research is an extension of information. In order to read research and understand it, the basics of the discipline must be understood. Think of research as an idea, which is analysed, synthesised and extended for its application.

Difficulty of material often necessitates more than one reading and thorough understanding of information.

Effective Reading Strategy

Preview the chapter before the lecture. Briefly look over titles, introduction, heading, subheadings, (few sentences about the subheadings), figures, diagrams, italicised or boldfaced terms and summaries. As you preview ask yourself-

- What this is all about?
- What do I know about this chapter and how much I have forgotten?

- What do I know about this chapter and how much I have forgotten?
- What is the organisational pattern of this chapter?
- How difficult or how easy this chapter is? Is there any terminology that is unfamiliar or that I will need to review?
- What are the parts I could skim and get the main idea?
- Where can I make logical breaks in the reading to judiciously divide my study time?
- In what order should I read the information in the chapter?
- Will it be easier and more motivating to read the most interesting section first?

Now, skim through the chapter but don't try to read it thoroughly yet. Just read the first and last sentences of paragraphs. Pull out some major ideas and details. Examine charts and figures. Try to understand the more important and frequently repeated terminology. Absorb the overall organisation of ideas. Don't panic or become overwhelmed with the readings. They may be dense, but not unconquerable. By previewing and skimming the materials before the lecture, you can clarify your doubts during the lecture and attain the level and depth of comprehension you really want to achieve.

If material is difficult and detailed and you have little or recent background in the discipline, it might be useful to review the fundamentals and basic terminology in an introductory text.

During the Lecture

In the classroom, be prepared to anticipate the information acquired from skimming your test book, and listen for clues during the lecture that will help you attain an appropriate level of comprehension when you read the same after it.

Take the notes on the left side of the page of your notebook and leave the right side of the page free to add related notes summarised from your textbook.

Read your textbook again after the lecture

Review and edit your notes taken from the lecture. Begin thinking about what additional information you'll need to add from the text to fill in the pages.

Read the relevant book content that you have previously skimmed.

CHAPTER -35

ABSENT-MINDEDNESS

People with excellent minds can also be absent minded. Here is a popular anecdote about absent- mindedness:

Louis Pasteur was dining at home with his friends. When his table companions were about to eat the grapes served for dessert, Pasteur stopped them saying, "There is nothing as dangerous as eating grapes without washing them first", and he washed his grapes in a glass of water. He then explained them all the bacilli and microbes that may be found in a cluster of grapes. Everybody listened raptly, but suddenly the spell was broken by a general burst of laughter. The scientist had unconsciously picked up the glass of water in which he had drowned so many germs and taken one long swallow. Pasteur was not the last to laugh at his absent mindedness.

So, absent-mindedness is nothing more than inattention. If we pay attention to anything, we will remember it.

Remember our eyes cannot see when our mind is absent.

Many a times we experience that when we start listening to a lecture in the class room with full attention but after sometime we find our mind wondering somewhere else.

Cure absentmindedness

To avoid the inattention and to concentrate on the class we should do the following things:

- It will be better if we read the chapter ourselves to get an idea, before the lecture.
- If we look at the teacher while the class is going on.
- If we write the brief notes or main words which will help us to grasp the whole lecture later on.
- If we clarify our doubts by asking the question in between or after the lecture.
- If we find our mind wondering we should immediately say to ourselves in our mind **LISTEN TO THE LECTURE.**
- Visualise the entire information to get a clear picture.
- Revise the information after the class.
- Revise the gists before the next class at home.

CHAPTER-36

PRACTICE RELAXATION

We are not a factory machine that automatically shuts down at the end of the day. Ironically we are not taught in the school how to shut down ourselves to restore our energy.

How many times do we hear students saying that they are relaxed physically but they feel mentally tired?

In order to accelerate our learning process we must be in the state of relaxation. According to Dr. James when we are relaxed our brain produces two chemicals endorphin and encephalo. Both the chemicals are phaline. Both the chemicals are good at producing positive feelings when our brain is positive. No doubt we find that we tend to remember less when we are tense and anxious. Many times we read a page over again and again but we don't grasp even a word simply,because we are worried about something.Whenever we are tensed our strengths become weakness and we lose confidence. Confidence is an important ingredient in learning. If we think we can, we can and this belief comes only from a relaxed mind.

To bring about the relaxation, we can go for the following exercises.

Breathing exercise

This is a very simple rule. Breathing should be as slowly as possible, so slowly that even we are not able to hear our incoming breadth. While breathing imagine that a feather is hanging by a thread from the ceiling about an inch from the nose. We should breathe out so slowly that in our imagination feather does not move or tremble.

Get rid of worry

The most important obstacle to relaxation is worry. Worry and anxiety freeze our conscious and subconscious mind preventing the learning process. Here is an exercise to control the worry.

Sitting comfortably in a peaceful place we should breathe normally and think about the matter worrying us. For an instance, if we are worrying about the approaching examination then we should think deeply about it. Now, we should think the very worst that can happen to us. Let us suppose the worst thing can be our failure in examination.

Now, we should feel anguish depression and disappointment and the pain in our chest and the feeling of fainting. Visualise getting a heart attack, and a doctor operating but not being successful in the operation.

Then listening to our heartbeat deliberately, we will realise that we are still alive and the worst which we visualised is never going to happen. So, we should make up our mind right now that most of the things we worry about are never going to happen in anyway, this is the worry that is more painful and agonising than what we are worried about.

Music

We can sit in a peaceful place and listen to music. Not all music is relaxing although it can be entertaining. Mostly people listen to music to relax. But, it has been seen that rock music and disco music produce a negative impact on the person .We can listen to baroque music for relaxation.

Physical Exercise

Physical exercises make our body and mind relaxed and alert Here some simple exercises are given-

Posture- Stand comfortably with your arms loosely hanging on your sides. Keep your back straight but relaxed.

Eyes-Keeping your head still, move your eyes to the right as far as they can go then back to centre. Move our eyes to left as far as they can go, then back to centre. Repeat both movements 10 times.

Neck-Breathing in, turn your neck slowly to the right. Breathing out, return your neck to the centre. Breathing in, turn your neck slowly to the left. Breathing out, return your neck to the centre. Repeat these two movements 10 times.

Arms- Breathing in, raise both arms above your head and stretch. Breathing out, drop both arms and loosen entire body. Do these two movements 10 times.

Shoulders- Breathing in normally, rotate both shoulders in a clockwise direction. Do this 10 times.

Waist- Put your hands on your waist. Breathing in,twist the upper part of your body to the right. Hold for 4 seconds. Breathing out, return to the centre. Breathing in, turn to the left, hold for 4 seconds. Breathing our return to centre position. Do this 10 times.

Thighs-Keeping your back straight, breathing in, lower yourself down to an imaginary chair. Holding your breath sit on this imaginary chair for 4 seconds. Breathing out, stand up slowly. Repeat 10 times.

Knees- Bend forward slightly and place your hands on your **Knee**. Feel the knobs of your knees with your palm. Press these kobs and rub them in a rotating motion to a count of 10. Straighten back to normal standing posture. Open your eyes.

Ankles-Breathing normally, lift your right foot slightly from the floor. Rotate your foot first clockwise 10 times, then anti-clockwise 10 times. Repeat this for the left foot.

Close your eyes. Breath normally. Take your gaze inward. Mentally travel down from your head to your toe. Then travel from your toe back to your head. This is a mental check to see that every muscle is relaxed.

Stretch-Breathing in deeply, and still keeping your eyes closed, lift both arms above your head and stretch. Imagine that you are a cat stretching. Then cross your arms and wrap them around yourself, giving yourself a big hug. Clasp tightly. Tighten clasp. Rock gently from side to side and say 'I love myself.' Say this 10 times. Open your eyes and feel marvellous.

We can find out our own ways to relax. Everybody has his own ways to relax. We can find them out, make a list and include them in our daily relaxation program.

What lies before us and what lies beyond us is tiny compared to what lies within us.

Henry David Thoreau

Bibliography

- Tony Buzen- Use Your Perfect Memory.
- Super Memory And Learning Skills- Bro. S. Augustine Paul.
- Organic Chemistry-Subhash Satish
- Mind Magic Kit- Dr. John Mumford
- Mind Body Power- Moni Lai Storz.
- More Anecdotes of The Great- J. Maurus
- Total Memory Workout- Cythia R. Green, Ph.D.